THE AGELESS CALL TO SERVE

Rethinking Military Service for a Changing World

LT. COL. LANNY SNODGRASS, MD, PHD

CASEMATE

Pennsylvania & Yorkshire

Published in the United States of America and Great Britain in 2024 by
CASEMATE PUBLISHERS
1950 Lawrence Road, Havertown, PA 19083, USA
and
47 Church Street, Barnsley, S70 2AS, UK

Hardcover Edition: ISBN 978-1-63624-417-4
Digital Edition: ISBN 978-1-63624-418-1

A CIP record for this book is available from the British Library

Printed and bound in the United Kingdom by CPI Group (UK) Ltd, Croydon, CR0 4YY
Typeset in India by DiTech Publishing Services

For a complete list of Casemate titles, please contact:

CASEMATE PUBLISHERS (US)
Telephone (610) 853-9131
Fax (610) 853-9146
Email: casemate@casematepublishers.com
www.casematepublishers.com

CASEMATE PUBLISHERS (UK)
Telephone (0)1226 734350
Email: casemate@casemateuk.com
www.casemateuk.com

Cover image and photo section: Courtesy of the Author.
Back flap image: Courtesy of Lawrence, Kansas, from Journal-World (January 2005).

With few exceptions individuals have been identified by pseudonyms to protect privacy and ensure anonymity. In some instances, location has also been altered.

Contents

To:
My wife
Tong Shen

My daughter
Saree Anne, mother of
my three grandchildren
Sydney, Tenleigh, and Brady

Foreword

Each journey, each life, weaves an intricate tapestry of courage, sacrifice, and wisdom. *The Ageless Call to Serve*, a compelling narrative by Dr. Lanny Snodgrass, conveys this realization and is a thought-provoking and intimate exploration of military service and mental health issues. Our shared human experience, accentuated by duty and service, is neither a linear path nor one confined by age limits.

As an Army Commander and psychiatrist, my career trajectory has given me a unique vantage point that intermingles military service with mental health expertise. From this intersection of experiences, I profoundly respect Dr. Snodgrass's *The Ageless Call to Serve*.

The first thread that catches my attention in Dr. Snodgrass's narrative tapestry is his courageous decision to join at 63. This bold move challenges the conventional wisdom surrounding age norms in the military. In a culture that often romanticizes the vigor of youth, Dr. Snodgrass asserts that experience, wisdom, and maturity are invaluable assets.

The enthusiasm of youth, while invaluable, often marries impulsivity, which in a theatre of conflict can transform into dire consequences. This statement isn't just a hypothesis—it's an observation I have made throughout my career. It's also alarming to see the ripple effect of untreated mental health issues post-active-duty spilling over into civilian life. Here, *The Ageless Call to Serve* shines a light, connecting the dots between age, impulsivity, and their psychological aftermath. Dr. Snodgrass's narrative navigates this maze with aplomb, offering profound insights that stem from personal experience and professional expertise.

The core premise of *The Ageless Call to Serve* forces us to question some entrenched notions. Are we unknowingly sacrificing the mental health of our young soldiers in our pursuit of national security? Could a shift in focus—towards valuing experience over youthful fervor—fundamentally transform the very fabric of our military, making it more effective?

The Ageless Call to Serve doesn't just ponder these questions but provides an enlightened pathway to understanding and answering them. Dr. Snodgrass offers a perspective that isn't merely that of a psychiatrist or a soldier. It's the perspective of a human being who has experienced the realities of war and its psychological aftermath.

As you read *The Ageless Call to Serve*, prepare for a journey that is as thought-provoking as enlightening. You will traverse a landscape of duty and service, wisdom and maturity, conflict and consequence. You'll be forced to confront uncomfortable truths about the hidden toll of war and the unseen costs of youthful impulsivity.

Most importantly, you'll witness a testament that in the realm of the military, duty can indeed call at any age. This book challenges us to redefine our perception of age, not as a barrier but as a potential strength in the theatre of war. It disrupts the preconceived notions of when a person should serve, suggesting a shift in focus towards when they should serve in combat, appreciating the diverse skills that older soldiers could provide.

In his narrative, Dr. Snodgrass masterfully weaves two professional realms that don't traditionally interact: psychiatry and the military. Yet, his exploration shows us that these fields aren't as disparate as they might initially appear. The psychological well-being of our soldiers is inextricably linked with their performance in the field, and acknowledging this connection is an urgent necessity.

The book also serves as an homage to all who serve—regardless of age. It portrays the military as an institution and a collective of unique individuals, each bringing skills, experiences, and perspectives. The depiction of the military as a dynamic entity capable of adapting, learning, and growing is a refreshing departure from the often-rigid portrayal of military life.

In my years of service and practice, I have witnessed our service members' immense resilience, adaptability, and grit firsthand. Yet, it's clear that we can do more to support them—especially when addressing the psychological impacts of service. As such, the lessons and insights offered in *The Ageless Call to Serve* are invaluable and essential.

Dr. Snodgrass's story is inspiring and captivating, resonating with anyone who has ever answered a call of duty. As you read, you will appreciate his unique perspective and the richness of his insights. I do not doubt that *The Ageless Call to Serve* will leave you with a deep understanding of the often-overlooked intersection between military service and mental health. It may also inspire you to join the conversation, to advocate for change, and to recognize the invaluable contribution that mature soldiers can make to our military.

As we look toward the future, it's clear that we must challenge our preconceived notions and adopt a more nuanced view of age and military service. In doing so, we can build a military that not only values the physical strength of youth but also appreciates the mental fortitude and wisdom that comes with age. *The Ageless Call to Serve* is an essential step on this journey—a call to action that we must all heed.

Richard L. Schneider, MD
Colonel, U.S. Army (Ret.)
Chief, Department, Psychiatry
Acting Commander, Madigan AMC

Preface

Wars may be unavoidable, but whom we choose to send into war zones is a matter very much up for debate. Like many great institutions, the U.S. military evolved to meet needs at critical moments. No doubt, if there ever were serious discussions about lowering or raising age limits, those debates ended decades ago. Such a discussion will now happen only if there is a grassroots movement. It is my great hope that this book will be a spark that lights a fire. With new technology forever changing how wars are fought, it is time to rethink whom we send into battle and whom we allow to join the military. The world continues to change and evolve, and the U.S. military needs to do the same.

In short, it's time for a change. It's time to acknowledge that people live longer, are generally healthier, that professional specialties are changing, and the nature of battle has changed, requiring fewer people on the field. It's also time for the U.S. military to acknowledge that recruiting and sending teenagers into a war zone is a bad idea. Such faulty thinking has resulted in an epidemic of suicides, depression, post-traumatic stress disorder (PTSD), and dishonorable discharges.

The 19-year-old soldier sitting in a trailer on an Army base in Colorado who launches a drone strike on an enemy target in the Middle East is probably as susceptible to PTSD as the soldier who fires a weapon during hand-to-hand combat. I've reviewed hundreds of PTSD cases and can categorically state that younger recruits are at much greater risk. Is it a risk worth taking?

In my career as a psychologist and later as a psychiatrist, I treated military personnel on foreign bases and eventually veterans at VA hospitals and U.S. Army casualty hospitals who suffered from PTSD, depression, suicidality, and a host of other war-related afflictions. I've seen up close what war does to people, especially those who are psychologically unfit to serve in the first place. I don't have all the answers, but I have some experience that allows me to offer suggestions and context for further discussion.

I do not advocate keeping teenagers from joining the military, but I think there is an argument to be made that teenagers should never be allowed on a battlefield. It is also time to remove upper-age restrictions, especially on licensed health professionals or any highly skilled professional that the military could use. This cause is particularly near and dear to my heart because at 63, I became one of the oldest persons to join the U.S. Army (first time) and go through officer basic training. As such, I believe I am the appropriate person to write about this—maybe the perfect individual to share a compelling testimony of someone who persisted and did not give up, broke the age ceiling, and reset the bar—the "Snodgrass example."

Even today, there remains in me a longing still to close the circle, to reunite with my fellow comrades, to again be part of that sacred battle buddy fraternity, of which civilian life has no substitute. If they would give me as little as one more day to serve, I would leap at the chance. I know that I am not alone in my commitment to our country. Millions of accomplished men and women over 40 with valuable skills would happily volunteer and serve if given a chance, and older individuals too, so long as they are capable and healthy.

We face a pivotal moment of reckoning. For too long, we have looked the other way as our youth suffered needless trauma in war while excluding older citizens who still have much to contribute. This hypocrisy must end.

With compassion and moral courage, we can create a military policy that fully values human dignity across the lifespan. But we must act swiftly, as challenges to U.S. national security mount. Each day that passes without reform means more lives are damaged, more potential wasted.

The men and women who serve of all ages deserve leadership wise enough to guide them justly. Anything less betrays their noble commitment. I hope this book will spur our institutions toward new thinking about military service that upholds America's highest ideals. The time is now to take action before further tragedy unfolds. Our troops, veterans, and nation await.

Part I
The Problem

CHAPTER I

Civilian to Soldier in Two Weeks

As the years pass, a road not taken may appear again as a distant byway if we're lucky. The journey along it, though previously unforeseen, may bring prodigious satisfaction. At least, this is how I felt after a miraculous opportunity to take on a new challenge, one that had eluded me when I was a boy, appeared before me in my golden years: to wear the uniform of an active-duty soldier in the U.S. military. This service would also satisfy a haunting lifelong passion for doing something honorable and noble for my country.

At 23, I had been deemed unfit for military service because of an injury from a meaningless high school football scrimmage. Nevertheless, I persisted, much as I have throughout my life, and eventually, against all odds, I seized the slim opportunity given to me months after the start of the second Gulf War. I proudly served my country as an Army officer for several great years. I would still be in the Army today had the government's rules and regulations not finally caught up with me at 68, thrusting a most unwelcome and forced separation upon me.

As I rounded 60 years, I had already invested 17 years in the Veterans Administration (VA) hospital system. In 2000, many, if not all, my colleagues would say I had arrived. I had a secure and high-paying salary on the final rung of GS (General Schedule) chief-level (VA), numerous educational achievements (BA, MS, PhD, MD), multiple languages (four), was happily married, and had an enviable pension waiting. Retirement was around the corner and would give me more time for my lifetime passion, playing piano, which sustained my soul through a doctoral program and medical school. I had put in so much time in so many areas perfecting myself, but to what end? To go to war? What was I thinking at age 60, knowing I had a sick heart in need of a pacemaker yet willing to risk it all? And if physical training was not going to be my Achilles' heel, surely one trip to the desert could be my bridge of no return.

In 1778, Samuel Johnson wrote, "Every man thinks meanly of himself for not having been a soldier, or not having been at sea." His words remain as true today as they were 250 years ago. The urge to serve our country is nearly all-pervasive. Even those who may appear to disdain military service may simply be projecting an outward hostility because they realize they missed the opportunity. It is easier to reconcile personal regret by being antagonistic to the idea.

Though I had greatly enjoyed my work as a psychiatrist healing profoundly wounded soldiers, I felt I had narrowly missed that elusive road, and it wouldn't be the first time. Over a decade earlier, I had gone overseas to work as a civilian doctor in Germany during the Gulf War. I had tried to convince myself that the experience would be rewarding enough to satisfy my longing to join the military, but it gave me no relief; in fact, it had the opposite effect. Perhaps it was my challenges with military hierarchy during 1991, my first year at the 98th General Hospital in Nuremberg, when I was thrust into a draining confrontation with the Pentagon and a four-star general. I won out in the end, but the struggle left me feeling I had something to prove to myself and the Army and that the only way to do it would be to enter their circle as an active-duty medical officer.

Standing outside the bubble made me feel like a raw man. Helping veterans was my life's work, but venturing into their sacred battle buddy space was impossible, as I had not earned the right. Sharing their histories of suffering and military life over many hours, days, and years affected how I saw myself, and I began to feel an inner void. I thought I had an obligation to them, myself, and my country. The discomfort chased me through most of my career. This sense eventually felt like subtle habituation. Those men and women who served had my deep admiration and undying respect, and I often tried to envision myself in their shoes, each one a hero in their right. A hero, alas, that I would never be. Or so I had believed.

★★★

At 62, I was diagnosed with a progressive cardiac problem called sick sinus syndrome. It caused my heart to stop and skip several beats for a few seconds at a time, prompting my heart rate to drop from the 70s to the 30s (beats per minute). Left untreated, the syndrome has a high mortality rate. The five-year survival rate is roughly 50 percent.

A year later, all this medical information was spelled out in a note my cardiologist sent to the Assistant to the Surgeon General of the Army at St. Louis Headquarters, including the recommendation that I get a pacemaker. The fact that I did not at that very moment have a pacemaker was critically important to the U.S. Army hierarchy, a bureaucracy that follows the rules to the letter, even when, at times, such rules may make little sense. By the Army's logic, if I had already had a pacemaker implanted, I would have been instantly disqualified from military service. People with pacemakers are, by definition, unfit for service, but apparently needing one and having one are worlds apart.

"Does the man have a pacemaker?"

"No."

"Well, then, no problem. He's good to go."

They cleared me without a hitch.

Thus began the realization of a dream that had been over 40 years in the making. I had volunteered to join the Army a little over three years earlier, sworn in 18 days past my 60th birthday, getting through the first steps in the process before things immediately stalled out. Someone in the chain of command noticed that even though I was a physician with a skill set the Army desperately wanted and needed, I was, well, 60. The mandatory removal date (MRD) for most officers (lieutenant colonel down to lieutenant) is the month of their 60th birthday. Here I was, trying to enter the Army at that age.

Different departments—Army HQ, St. Louis, Fort Knox Army HQ—judged my application in different ways, none of which led to a decision about whether I should be admitted or not. Each time I inquired about my status I got a different answer. The lieutenant colonel (LTC) in Fort Knox refused to recommend a mandatory removal date (MRD) extension; I was too old. However, on May 1, 2001, the Reserve Coordinator for Western Regional Medical Command (WRMC) took up my cause and advised the LTC, "Snodgrass is going for a Congressional, and I am supporting it." She saw my potential value to the Army and pushed hard for an age waiver. "This soldier is in a critical specialty ... why we are MRDing a newly commissioned critically short physician."

Without her unwavering support, there is no doubt that my candidacy would have been a complete non-starter. She was unable to pierce through the bureaucracy, but her many conversations with various staff at the Pentagon kept my candidacy alive—barely. An appeal would be waiting for two years for approval from the Secretary of the Army. The constant shifts in tone of their correspondence, which fluctuated between hopeful, hopeless, and then back to hopeful, made me think that the U.S. Army had a collective thought process in place for challenging the finality of decisions and this one was plagued by ambivalence.

For three years, my papers ended up in the Army's version of purgatory, in a file, and on the desk of someone who lacked the authority to make a clear-cut decision. As the years passed, I gradually accepted that I would never achieve my dream.

During the initiation of a conflict that sent 130,000 U.S. soldiers to Iraq on March 20, 2003, it became apparent to the U.S. military that its psychiatric staff was spread woefully thin, prompting a newfound enthusiasm for any qualified candidates who might bolster the team. And so, in December 2003, orders to report to Fort Sam Houston showed up most unexpectedly in my mailbox. My hands trembled a little as I read the words I had, for so many years, longed to read. My amygdala sent a clear message to my frontal lobe: HOLY CRAP! I'm joining the U.S. Army!

"You are ordered to report for active duty training (ADT) for the period shown. On completion of the period of ADT, unless sooner released or extended by proper authority, you will return to the place where you entered ADT."

Given that the United States had just gone to war, I realized that my late induction into the military was done entirely out of necessity. With the Selective Service System suspended since 1975, there was no draft or mandatory service requirement. This meant that, at that moment, the United States urgently needed qualified medical personnel, especially psychiatrists, no matter where they could find them. Had it not been for the war in Iraq and a medical corps that had dwindled considerably since the Vietnam War, I am quite sure that my orders would have eventually gone into a circular file. At that moment, however, the United States had a dire hole to fill, and I was one of the few in my profession available to fill it.

At the same time, to say I was stunned would be a significant understatement. I had little time to prepare physically or emotionally. Not only was I a good 25 pounds heavier than I wanted to be, but my level of cardio fitness was pathetic. Climbing a set of stairs left me winded—not precisely what you'd call fighting form. I was worried I might become a laughingstock, or worse, a humiliated and abject failure to be held up for ridicule by my medical and professional peers.

Because I had volunteered, and because I was already a licensed physician with many years of experience, I was told I would join the U.S. Army at the rank of major, but only if I first passed a rigorous and grueling two-week basic training camp designed specifically for med corps officers. As I reread the Army's letter for perhaps the tenth time, an admonition given by my father when I was 12 rang out in my mind: "Be careful what you wish for because you might just get it."

I awoke at 2:00am, with skipped heartbeats, obsessively counting them for several minutes. The skips came in clusters, with three and a quarter seconds between them; each ventricular contraction came with such force that it felt like my heart was trying to come out of my chest. On the evening of January 3, 2004, the final night before my departure for basic training, I caught only four hours of uninterrupted sleep.

My flight to San Antonio was uneventful. The basic training my seatmate and I were scheduled to attend was designed to be more rigorous and intense than usual—a condensed version necessitated by the war. For the other 199 attendees, it would essentially be a refresher course. If someone had to lay odds on who would be most likely to drop out, there's no question I would be the heavy favorite.

Welcoming seniors to basic training (OBC) brings a unique challenge to the training environment. Being the oldest senior (age 63) among 199 other servicemembers, most of whom were nearly half my age, presented awkward moments for me on my first day. Although the military is accustomed to working with individuals of various ages and backgrounds, a 63-year-old joining the ranks of the 187th Alpha Company added a new layer of camaraderie to the culture.

Having been commissioned to a higher rank (Major) than most, did not offer me much solace. I was green and they knew it. As first glance, they were cordial, but the age-chasm gave way to awkwardness and skepticism.

My first wakeup call came in the morning report for duty. The command divided all members into squads of 10 to 12 each. The nuance of feeling like I was not in the circle of the "good ole boys" club was palpable after it was time to choose battle buddies—I was left out. I felt I was a misfit among a squad of surrogate daughters and sons. I soon discovered Vickie, a 32-year-old, who had also been left unpaired. We were paired by default, a far cry from ideal. She stood sleek and sturdy, with a figure fit for a long-distance runner. As we gazed briefly at each other with first-name introductions, I begged for a hint of a smile or at least some indication of acceptance. At first blush, I saw only a message that read, "Oh well, if it has to be, let it be!"

That afternoon meeting was our formal introduction to basic training. It began with a greeting from a lieutenant colonel, who explained that "We are the sum of our decisions, and there are four decisions which may get you into trouble." First was fraternization: as an officer, you must not have relationships with enlisted personnel (i.e., anything romantic). Next was cheating and plagiarizing; then drunk driving—this guts careers, so conduct yourself accordingly. Finally there was the diagnostic APFT (the Army Physical Fitness Test)—if you are not in the best shape, start running on your own time.

Then the lieutenant colonel gave us the lowdown on the Diagnostic PT test. Soldiers were advised on the scoring standards for each portion of the test; my minimum passing score would be 60, calibrated to my age. We were instructed to carry a scorecard to each event. There would be push-ups and sit-ups, then a 10-minute recovery period, followed by a 2.5-mile run (five laps around the track). As a bunch of other tests and requirements were spelled out, my mind began to spin. It occurred to me that I should have started getting into shape for this test at least six months earlier.

That afternoon it was back to lecture time. The first topic of discussion was the changes in the Army medical corps protocols. In previous wars, we learned, access to med-corps companies was too far from the frontlines of battle, placing the wounded at great risk because they didn't have immediate access to urgent medical treatment. Changes were now being made to move the companies closer to the frontlines to be available more quickly to help save more soldiers' lives. We learned that CCPs (casualty collecting points) were now located closer to CSHs (combat support hospitals) to ensure nearby pickup and transfers of the wounded. This information explained why psychiatrists were stationed in Baghdad; there was a 92-bed CSH there.

We were told that 100 percent of the previous month's OBC class had been sent to Iraq. As I heard this, I went electric, shocked to my senses. Holy crap, what am I doing here? I wasn't sure, with my heart condition, that I could survive a deployment to Iraq, with its harsh conditions, unforgiving terrain, days of unending 130-degree-plus days, and humidity that could suck the life out of energy itself. We had just been informed that aid stations would be available. But what if I had a syncopal episode (loss of consciousness from insufficient blood flow to the brain) or needed emergency surgery with pacemaker leads attached to my heart? I was quite sure that no field hospital existed in Iraq with specialists able to treat me. My cardiologist said my chances of having syncope while driving down the freeway were one in 200. And now, an assignment to the desert was more likely than ever. Well, at least I wasn't going to be driving a tank.

It was time to take the PT test. We stood ready to be graded by Captain Star or a sergeant who hovered over us from above. He bent over our bodies as we performed each exercise, ensuring that we didn't dare do them wrong. The temperature was chilling cold from the north wind gusts piercing our skin.

Then came the shocker: an order to "Take off your jackets!" They wanted to ensure we couldn't cheat when performing our push-ups.

The sergeant peered intensely as we performed each rep, his head near the turf, to ensure our shoulders were parallel to the ground (not touching it). This was to rule against any observational error and to decide whether a push-up qualified or was disqualified, depending on the sergeant's judgment and eyesight.

We were given two minutes to complete this feat. I performed 35 push-ups, but the sergeant wouldn't count my first one because my knees were on the ground when he said, "Start." Nonetheless, I gave it my all, and on the 36th attempt, I fell to the ground, completely winded.

Then came the sit-ups. My feet were held by the other older officer candidate, a 52-year-old orthopedic surgeon with prior military experience and boundless energy. "Man, you're doing great! That's great!" he told me after each rep. I blacked out or lost track at 20.

The run was next. Have I mentioned that the wind chill was severe? Just as I lined up, I suddenly became fully aware that I was sick, that horrible moment when the brain acknowledges a series of symptoms that can no longer be ignored. My nose, throat, and bronchia felt like they were being assaulted by a barrage of inflammatory responses. I pulled my zipper jacket tightly over my mouth and most of the way up to my nose. My upper respiratory status had been compromised. I don't think anyone had a clue about the issues with my heart or whether I would be able to perform sufficiently under stress, given my low baseline and skipped beats.

The captain called for the 2.5-mile run, five laps around the track. He watched me and heard me call out to him as I passed by after each half mile: "Star one ..., Star two ..., Star three ..., Star four ..., Star five."

In the last lap, to my embarrassment, I saw 198 comrades of Alpha Company standing shivering in the cold and waiting for me to finish. Some were sitting in the bleachers along the sideline. I was also feeling quite embarrassed, but less so when the unexpected happened: I discovered a 55-year-old African American officer in our company was just behind me—number 199.

When I had started the run, as I was halfway around my first lap, I saw him fall to the side of the track and wail in pain with an injured ankle. On this last lap, he was giving it his all. He was coming down the final stretch, and I tried to speed up, but so did he, while limping on his one leg.

I did not want to be last, but for an instant, I felt pity for the poor guy; I did not have the heart to outdo him. Classmates all shouted as Captain Star called out "44" (as in minutes). There was no pride in this performance, but at least I was going to finish. I eased up at the end to join shoulders with my company mate. We crossed the finish line together, 199 and 200, tied for last place.

Following PT training and testing, the afternoon lecturer, Captain Stern, had the frankness of a bulldog and a prominent forehead and nose that completed the comparison. He spoke with abject insensitivity toward psychiatric services, which shocked me. He possessed a primitive crudeness in his perception of mental health treatment and commented against using psychiatric services, "Little use, if any." Furthermore, he stated, "I will send exactly none of my soldiers to see a psychiatrist. If they go crazy, I just hit them in the head, knock them out, and send them out of my unit." He sounded like General Patton 2.0. Actually, this was possibly even more ruthless than how Patton treated his troops.

...to be continued.

CHAPTER 2

Age and Military Service

The best efforts of military men to de-glamorize war have failed and probably always will. The most famous admonition was given in 1879 by Civil War General William Tecumseh Sherman in front of 10,000 onlookers at the Michigan Military Academy graduation ceremony. "War is Hell!" instantly became a famous dictum. Still, the original context and the rest of his words went missing; for example, "It is only those who have neither fired a shot nor heard the shrieks and groans of the wounded who cry aloud for blood, for vengeance, for desolation."

Over the decades, young people who heard the phrase foolishly decided to embrace war instead of rejecting it. "War is Hell" became interpreted as "War is glorious." Since well before the Civil War, joining the military at a young age served as a rite of passage, a way for men (and later women) to prove their bravery, fortitude, and boldness. Sherman tried, but ultimately failed, to convince young men to avoid battlefields. One hundred fifty years later, young people still join the military at age 18 (17 with parental consent), and too many of them wind up as a statistic—KIA (killed in action).

We might look to the history of war to find the justification and rationale for sending young men, boys really, as the burden bearer to soldier the main thrust of the battle. How did we get here, and why did we arrive at a specific age for youth to join the military?

Looking back into ancient history, in Sparta boys were trained from a young age to become warriors. At seven, boys were taken from their families and placed into military training camps, where they were taught to fight and endure harsh conditions. By age 20, these boys were expected to become full-time soldiers and join the army.

In England, during the Middle Ages, men who wanted to better their situation in life could sign up to serve their ruler or lord in the military in a practice that we now refer to as a feudal society. William I introduced the idea into England after the Battle of Hastings in 1066. Simply put, in exchange for service, the ruler gave fighters (who became known as vassals or knights) a "fief"—a unit of land that came with as many as 30 (unfree) peasant families who worked the land. Service typically consisted of 40 days' service in peacetime and indefinite service during war. There were considerable complexities to the system, but essentially the deal was land as a reward for military service. The system lasted for many centuries, following which direct cash payment instead of land became the norm.

Most knights in the feudal society were at least 21 years old. The minimum age for soldiers was generally thought to be 16, but most were allowed, maybe even encouraged, to fight until they were in their 60s or at such a point that they became too fragile or frail. Archeological digs in Britain found that the average age of most medieval soldiers was approximately 29 (Nicholson, 2004: 82).

In time, the minimum and maximum age for service appears to have evolved according to needs and available manpower. British soldiers in regiments stationed in America before and during the American Revolution were generally at least 30 years old. According to one study, only 1 percent of soldiers were younger than 20, and 21 percent were older than 40 (Rodger, 2004).

In early America, qualifications for enlistment in military service varied and changed over time. The original standards for the Continental army stated that individuals were not to be enlisted after 30 years of age, nor less than 5 feet 5 inches high, but growing lads of 17–19 years of age could be enlisted at 5 feet 4 inches. These would be amended during the War of 1812 to permit infantrymen enlisting between the ages of 17 and 30, with a height requirement of at least 5 feet 6 inches. However, growing lads aged 17 to 19 could be enlisted if they were no less than 5 feet 5 inches.

Notably, there was no upper age limit for service, meaning that individuals of any age could join the military. At the other extreme, even boys as young as 12 were considered for service, although they were mainly assigned roles such as drummers or medics. During the War of 1812, there was an incentive for recruitment, with a $16 bonus and three months' pay promised to those who enlisted. Additionally, they were offered 160 acres of land after fulfilling their duty obligations.

During the Revolutionary War, the Continental army faced many challenges, including a lack of experienced soldiers. After the war, authorities realized that having experienced soldiers was crucial for an effective military force. They often relaxed the age and height requirements to encourage veterans and former soldiers to continue serving.

In 1860, the Confederacy enacted a conscription law, requiring all white males between 18 and 33 to serve for three years in the military. Three years later, the limits were expanded to include all males between 17 and 50. The Civil War Military Draft Act of 1863 mandated the enrollment of every male citizen between the ages of 20 and 45 to the Confederate army. This pattern continued with the Spanish–American War of 1898, as Congress enacted a law requiring all males between 18 and 45 to be designated for conscription.

During World War I, the Selective Training and Service Act of 1917 required all males between the ages of 21 and 30 to register for service. The National Defense Act of the 1920s established policies for voluntary enlistment. In 1940, Congress modified the Selective Service and Training Act, mandating that all males between 21 and 35 register for the draft when the military services' numbers fell below the minimum requirement.

During the Cold War in 1948, President Truman requested the reinstatement of the draft. The new Selective Service Act required men between 19 and 26 to serve 12 months of active duty. In the Korean War, males aged 18½ to 35 were called to serve active duty for two years. It was President Nixon in 1969 who enacted the 19-year-old draft. This change meant that if a male had not been drafted by age 19, he would be exempt from military service unless in the event of war or national emergency.

Presently, the U.S. maintains an all-volunteer armed force, with all male citizens aged 18 to 26 required to register for the draft. They remain subject to training service until the age of 35. There has been a movement to include females and all citizens in the draft qualifications. Advocates for including females and all citizens in the draft qualifications argue that women have proven themselves to be just as capable as men in the military and that excluding them from the draft is a form of discrimination. Such countries, such as Israel, Norway, and Sweden, have already implanted gender-neutral conscription policies.

Overall, the qualifications for enlistment in military service in America have evolved and adapted to the changing needs and circumstances of the nation. The policies have ultimately changed from varying age and height requirements to conscription laws and the reinstatement of the draft.

Throughout history, age limits for various activities and responsibilities have shifted during times of war. During the Napoleonic Wars, both France and Britain lowered the minimum age for sailors. In Britain, the age limit was reduced from 18 to 16, and in France, it was lowered from 18 to 15. This move increased the number of sailors available for naval warfare. Age limits have been lowered during other wars due to the perception of increased maturity or capability in younger individuals, and the desire to honor the sacrifices made by older generations. In addition to this, throughout history determined teenagers have managed to join up despite not yet meeting the minimum age requirements.

During the American Civil War, underage soldiers were common on both sides. Many boys lied about their age to join the Army and fight for their cause. Some estimates suggest that as many as 20 percent of all Civil War soldiers were under 18 (McPherson, 1998).

In the United Kingdom, during World War I, the age limit for military service was initially set at 18, then was lowered to 16. The change was partly because many young men were eager to join the war effort and prove their bravery and patriotism but also because the need for soldiers was so great. Some young men even lied about their age to join the military, creating more stringent age-verification measures. Many countries also raised the age limit for military service during World War I. In the United States, for example, the age limit was increased from 31 to 40, and in Germany, it was raised from 45 to 50. This change was deemed necessary because many young men had already been conscripted, and older men were needed to fill the gaps.

During World War II, older men were often encouraged to enlist or take on other roles supporting the war effort. In the United States, for example, the age limit for military service was initially set at 21, which was later raised to 35. The change was partly due to the fact that many older men had already gained valuable experience and skills and were seen as capable of contributing in various ways, such as serving as instructors or working in support roles.

During World War II, many young girls were conscripted to serve as nurses and other support roles in Japan. These girls, known as "comfort women," were often as young as 12 or 13 and were forced to serve in terrible conditions. Also, during World War II, the age limit for enlistment in the United States Navy was initially set at 17 but was later lowered to 16 due to a shortage of manpower and the need for more sailors to serve on ships.

When recruitment shortages grew acute in World War II, Britain formed "Dad's Army," which enlisted veterans aged 40–70 into the Home Guard. These older soldiers maintained coastal lookouts, provided local defense, and completed support duties to free younger troops for combat. Their contributions were praised as indispensable. Japan's "Patriotic Citizens Fighting Corps" took an even more radical approach, conscripting all healthy males aged 15–60 into civil defense roles. Elderly soldiers were deployed in suicidal attacks or strapped with explosives for kamikaze missions. The physical stamina required for such missions would be significant and under extreme duress. It is important to consider whether they were acting on their own free will or coercion. Many, if not most were subject to intense ideological indoctrination and pressure by the military of that time.

The average age of the Marines who fought in the Battle of Iwo Jima in 1945 was 22. By comparison, the age range of the Japanese fighters was 14–60. The tragic human losses in wartime can result in mandating lower age requirements to replace the depleted ranks. Desperation in a losing war can show no mercy. Morality becomes skewed, and death becomes the ultimatum regardless of age.

In Norway, during World War II, many 16-year-olds participated in youth movements, which often provided physical fitness and training in martial arts. Some of these youth movements were anti-German and worked alongside the larger resistance when ranks were depleted (Tonder, 1981). Their involvement highlights their courage and dedication to their country during the German occupation.

During the Korean War, the United States Army lowered its age limit for volunteers from 18 to 17 to increase the pool of potential soldiers and to make up for the high casualty rates that the Army was experiencing.

Expediency and the need for more extensive military reserves during conflict have also prompted unpopular age changes. In Israel today, for example, military service is mandatory for all citizens over 18. However, there are exceptions for those deemed too old or young to serve. For example, men over 27 and women over 24 are generally not required to serve, while men and women can begin military service as young as 18.

During the Vietnam War, the United States lowered the age limit for military service from 21 to 18. This was controversial at the time, as many people felt that if 18-year-olds were old enough to fight and die for their country, they should be old enough to vote. The 26th Amendment, known as "old enough to fight, old enough to vote," was signed into law by President Nixon on July 5, 1972. This amendment stated that the voting age should be set at 18, aligning it with the draft age.

During the Falklands War in 1982, the British Army allowed soldiers as young as 17 to enlist and serve in combat roles. The age limit was lowered to increase the number of troops available for the conflict, which was fought against Argentina over control of the Falkland Islands.

More recently, following 9/11, many American veterans well past typical service age volunteered to reenlist, compelled by a sense of duty. Their technical skills and leadership qualities honed over long careers could have provided invaluable support during the War on Terror. Unfortunately, regulations largely prohibited their return, and a precious reservoir of experience was left untapped due to ageism.

All the above examples demonstrate that age limits have always been arbitrary and malleable. When it serves the greater good, arguments will be raised to raise and lower age limits to increase the pool of qualified candidates. Moreover, in a recent article by Metzel Getty from *Times of London* (July 18, 2023), this is brought to the forefront, noting Russia has now increased the maximum age to 70 for men to be mobilized to fight on the frontlines in Ukraine, due to the vast numbers of Russian soldiers killed since the invasion of Ukraine.

★★★

If you were to ask random people on the street in the U.S., most would probably tell you that the lower age of 18 and the upper age of 65 are enshrined in some important document. Such is not the case. Although the U.S. military has endlessly studied the minutiae of war, the institution suffers from severe myopia. To my knowledge, there has never been a study about the military's upper and lower age limits. Indeed, in the past 50 years, no Pentagon general or congressional committee has even considered age or other screening criteria. For whatever reason, the topic is not one that any senior official in the military sees as an urgent mandate that needs attention. What was good enough in 1971 is still good enough in 2024. We live in an era when looking at brain development instead of chronological years to screen candidates is possible. We also have the means to extensively test people before service to exclude or include candidates, regardless of age. Despite those advantages, the U.S. military still relies on rules and regulations established nearly 50 years ago.

Joining the military is often depicted as an adventure. Indeed, some older veterans argue in favor of teens enlisting in the military to serve in a war, like former German soldier Roland Bartetzko. He fought with Croatians in the Bosnian War. He said age 19 is perfect for an infantry soldier because "you won't feel any back pain after you've slept for three weeks in a forest … you're impressionable and won't criticize your commander's decision. You also don't know how extremely precious life is. You'll be more ready to risk it than someone who is 30 years of age." Captain Jeff Bamberg, who served in the USAF for eight years, agrees. "The upside of having younger, less fully developed intellectual people is that your brain still hasn't kicked in to understand that everything is there to kill you. You feel invincible, and you can go out and do the things that military people need to do."

Other veterans would disagree with him and offer no justification for 18- and 19-year-old soldiers to be placed at the combat front, who thought they were "cannon fodder," as a Vietnam veteran commander quoted. In a 2023 interview, John P., who enlisted at age 17 to fight in the Vietnam War, serving one year and then another year to spare his older brother from deployment, said, "I was young and didn't know anything, I was stupid... Hell No." Vietnam-era veteran LTC Crile Doscher sees it this way in a 2022 interview: "They are totally fearless at that age. And maybe they don't have the greatest judgment they will have in their lifetime, but they are fearless... it's not the nicest age in the world. It's your child."

As a medical doctor, psychiatrist, and therapist, I have treated numerous individuals whose lives were deeply scarred by their experiences serving in the military at a young age. These men and women carried the weight of their service throughout their lives. There are countless reasons why the policy of sending teenagers to fight wars is flawed, and if it were up to me, I would never permit such decisions.

However, I recognize that I am fighting an uphill battle. Veterans and military leaders with whom I have spoken unanimously acknowledge the issue. Still, they also emphasize that because teenagers lack a full understanding of the risks and long-term consequences, they are willing to charge into battle bravely. These young people are needed to defend us, as they are less likely to question orders or retreat from an imminent threat.

While I do not have the authority to make policy decisions, it is essential for those who do to grasp the long-term consequences. Sending young people into perilous situations for which they are psychologically and mentally unprepared can lead to adverse outcomes. PTSD, depression, suicide, and self-destructive behavior are just a few of the long-term challenges faced by these individuals. Although we appreciate their service, we must also consider the lasting price that both they and society must bear.

Studies have found that younger soldiers are more susceptible to developing PTSD, related to higher rates of experienced trauma and insufficient coping mechanisms (Shea et al., 2013). In a recent study by Dohrenwend et al. (2013), it was discovered that soldiers who enlisted before the age of 25 and served in combat were seven times more likely to develop PTSD syndrome than their cohorts who were 25 or older. This research also showed when adding two additional factors (problems in childhood and harming the innocent) would increase their risk of developing PTSD following combat to a 97 percent chance. Addressing moral injury—spiritual, psychological, or emotional harm experienced due to a moral conflict—is crucial when discussing the morality of sending young individuals into combat (Litz et al., 2009). This ethical burden can be lifelong, affecting relationships, mental health, and the ability to reintegrate into society.

While there may be military necessities for lowering age limits in times of war, we cannot ignore the psychological and moral implications. As a society, we must strive to fully understand the impact on young lives and take measures to support them before, during, and after their service. Though victories may be won on the battlefield, healing the invisible wounds of war remains an ongoing struggle. Our youth deserve our deepest care and wisdom as they take up this solemn duty.

CHAPTER 3

The Price We Pay for Sending Teenagers to War

Gas! Gas! Quick, boys! —An ecstasy of fumbling,
Fitting the clumsy helmets just in time;
But someone still was yelling out and stumbling
And flound'ring like a man in fire or lime...
Dim, through the misty panes and thick green light,
As under a green sea, I saw him drowning.

In all my dreams, before my helpless sight,
He plunges at me, guttering, choking, drowning.

If in some smothering dream you too could pace
Behind the wagon that we flung him in,
And watch the white eyes writhing in his face,
His hanging face, like devil's sick of sin;
If you could hear at every jolt the blood
Come gargling from the froth-corrupted lungs,
Obscene as cancer, bitter as the cud
Of vile, incurable sores on innocent tongues, —
My friend, you would not tell with such high zest
To children ardent for some desperate glory.
The old lie: *Dulce et decorum est.*
Pro patria mori [Death is sweet and beautiful].
—"DULCE ET DECORUM EST" ("IT IS SWEET AND FITTING"),
BY WILFRED OWEN (1918)

It was 1971. The Vietnam War raged with a ferocity that hadn't been seen since the end of World War II. America needed every able-bodied soldier it could find, as long as they met the minimum age and physical requirements. George was one such recruit, drafted out of high school at 18 and sent to fight on the frontlines right after basic training.

Higher-ups in the U.S. Army command in Vietnam discovered that George was a diamond in the rough. He was certifiably brilliant, the valedictorian of his high school class, who spoke seven languages fluently, including, fortuitously, Vietnamese. Given those facts and that he was Filipino and looked, according to his superiors, "vaguely Vietnamese," they thought he'd do well gathering local intelligence. Put simply, George's mission was to cross into enemy territory, chat up soldiers in bars, and report to the U.S. Army with any meaningful information—all without raising any red flags. Later in his military service, with the wholehearted support of his superior officers, he posed as a household servant and worked for a high-ranking North Vietnamese official. It was, of course, a perilous and potentially lethal assignment. Getting caught would undoubtedly mean being charged with espionage, resulting in instant execution.

George made it through two tours of duty and two full years of service in Vietnam before his luck finally ran out. Unfortunately, he asked the wrong person the wrong question at the wrong time. He was brought first to a police station and then to a North Vietnamese military camp under suspected espionage.

Given the nature of his job, it wasn't unusual for George to go silent for weeks at a time. On this occasion, however, George's absence was noted after no one had heard from him for a month. With no indication that he might have been captured, the U.S. Army incorrectly assumed George had gone AWOL. They sent the Criminal Investigation Department (CID) to his young wife's house to question her about his whereabouts. The encounter left her deeply shaken. She knew only that George wasn't AWOL because he would never abandon her or their one-year-old daughter, which meant he had to have been captured or he was dead. Friends and family later reported that after that encounter, George's wife was never the same. She became a chain smoker and lived in constant, incapacitating fear for the rest of her life.

By the time the North Vietnamese incorrectly decided George was not a spy, he had been held captive, beaten, and tortured for months. Finally, he snuck back across enemy lines, returned to his unit, and, after a debriefing, was sent back home with an honorable discharge.

His military service was over, but the war never ended for George. For the next two decades, his life was consumed by what his son called "constant flashbacks," better known as PTSD symptoms. It consumed his thoughts and vexed his soul while corroding hope and stealing his dignity. To numb the pain or erase the memories of his military service, he drank heavily every day, without exception, and often to the point of stupor. Of course, George had difficulty holding down a steady job, was a mostly absent father in his children's lives, and became a threat to his local community. On at least two occasions, police were called to quell disturbances at his house when George brandished a gun in sight of his neighbors. He eventually sought treatment at the VA hospital for the toxic combination of Agent Orange exposure and chronic alcoholism, but it was too late. He died at the age of 41.

Was George, at 18, too young to serve? Adolescents often do not have the capacity to understand and process fear; denial is a common response, a lie that is repeated over and over. "I'm fine..." But how does this work as a combat soldier when one is in harm's way? There may not be a perfectly suitable age to serve in the military or military combat, but many who served in a war zone, like George, were damaged for the remainder of their lives. The majority of veterans who served in Iraq and Afghanistan are currently in their 30s and 40s. This age profile aligns with the peak years for mental health conditions to surface, further substantiating the prevalence of PTSD among this demographic. Moreover, the age profiles of veterans who have taken their own lives also align with these age groups, highlighting the correlation between military service, mental health struggles, and suicide. The statistics speak for themselves, as noted by J. L. Liebert and W. J. Birnes in *Wounded Minds* (2013): "A US military veteran commits suicide every 65 minutes... 1 in 5 veterans who served in Iraq and Afghanistan have PTSD... Half of those veterans never seek treatment."

Brain Maturation and Developmental Markers

Over the past 40 years, I have met thousands of young people, aged 18 to 25, who were either in the Army or wanted to be. Yet, as dissimilar as all these individuals were, there is a common thread: they all grew up. It should come as no surprise to anyone that people's ideas and impressions at 18 are often not the same as when they turn 25. At 18, most individuals are at the upper end of their developmental continuum (that phase of life development between 10 and 19). Such maturation is a normal part of development from adolescence to adulthood. For example, even though it is legal, with parental consent, to marry at the age of 14 in Alaska or 15 in Maryland, Hawaii, and Kansas, very few such unions happen—and for a good reason. According to statistics compiled by a divorce law firm, 48 percent of those who marry before the age of 18 are likely to divorce within 10 years, compared to 25 percent of those who marry after age of 25 (McKenzie Law Firm, 2022).

Similarly, a well-known and respected research study tracked the career interest of a large group of students from age 18 to 25 and found that their "likes and dislikes" changed by 50 percent during those seven years (Strong, 1943). Stability of interests studies by Swanson and Hansen (1988) reveals by age 25 interests are very stable, which then allows counselors to have confidence in a test score, e.g., the Strong test, to be used to predict future behaviors. J. Round and R. Su, writing about the power of interests (2014), offer several reasons why interests are such strong predictors of career choices. First, interests reflect an individual's passions and preferences, providing insight into what kinds of activities and subjects they are naturally drawn to. When individuals choose to pursue a major and occupation that align with their interests, they are more likely to feel engaged and motivated in their work. This enthusiasm often translates into higher levels of performance and job satisfaction.

When sending teens to military combat, one must consider developmental markers. According to S. B. Johnson's neuroimaging studies report (2009), "The adolescent brain continues to develop into the early twenties." This medical fact raises an issue for policymakers, particularly for the military, to reconsider the age at which young military recruits are ready to bear arms in combat. Moreover, if teenagers are legally considered less culpable for criminal behavior, are they a reliable risk to be ordered into military action?

The Air Guard has introduced a preliminary approach which provides a camp experience for prospective high school recruits. In their senior year, they enter a group experience of assimilation. No one wants a battle buddy who cannot have their back. Social psychologist Professor Omri Gillath has concluded that those with an insecure attachment style have issues relating to trust and closeness (Gillath et al., 2016).

The prefrontal cortex in the human brain performs many critical functions: reasoning, planning, judgment, and impulse control. These functions are essential to becoming an adult. Considering that the prefrontal cortex is not developed fully until the early 20s, this raises questions about risks that these young men may present to themselves and others, as well as about their judgment, which is required in the face of combat with the enemy. It also calls into question moral issues on several levels for the military to reexamine; for instance, in the heat of battle, if the logical rationale for decision-making is not yet fully developed, what might this mean for one who has to make life-changing decisions?

With an underdeveloped prefrontal cortex, denial (refusal to admit the truth or reality of something unpleasant) and impulsivity can be dangerous. Young service members may misjudge the potential danger of encounters with the enemy. It is characteristic of late adolescent behavior to present themselves as confident even when they are not. Feelings of overconfidence can overshadow their perception of potential threats. The inability to know the difference between what a service member perceives as real and what is occurring in combat can make the difference between survival and death. Confusion can be a product of impulsivity.

Most mental health clinicians consider denial as a weak defense mechanism. However, it is part of normal brain development and is the process of evolving into a complete developmental phase. This mechanism involves denying the consequences of reality. In her "Five Stages of Grief Model," Elizabeth Kübler Ross names denial as one of those five stages, an unconscious and self-protective mechanism.

Defense mechanisms allow us to pretend that shock has not taken place. Sigmund Freud emphasized denial as an ego-protecting mechanism. The danger of overreliance on this mechanism can limit reality checks and lead to lying to oneself in the fray of combat.

Historically, wars have generally been fought by combat troops in their late teens whose identity is still developing. Combat trauma experiences become self-absorbed and inadequately processed, affecting one's emotions, thoughts and a sense of self. This combination brings forth confusion, which can alter a young person's personality, still in a growth phase.

Although character development occurs throughout adult life, severe or prolonged war trauma takes its toll on the process. This medical observation is aptly stated by Ursano et al. (2010) in the article "PTSD and Destruction." He expands on this idea, identifying disasters that can arrest personality and may occur with exposure to near death or witnessing the death of other comrades, which results in survivor's guilt or illusions. "I'm responsible, I killed that soldier, or I should have saved him… The perceptions of oneself in the face of military combat, especially for adolescents, are subject to breakdown of denial, resulting in demoralized, weak coping capabilities." Ursano believes that this, in turn, causes them to regress and harken back to early reminders of their frailty, vulnerability, and incompleteness of who they really are and accentuates the struggle for their search for identity.

A late 2022 *New York Times* release of a video of the atrocities in Bucha, Ukraine, portrayed the inhumane side of war that youth encounters. The film "Caught on Camera, Traced by Phone: The Russian Military Unit That Killed Dozens in Bucha," documents footage of soldiers in the act of committing war crimes, although there is no doubt that such events have likely occurred in every war since the dawn of human history. Noted by one commentator on seeing the film, "But, look at men (young men, always men) from any nation, in any war or fighting situation, and one will see beastly behavior—some of it, gruesomely, even encouraged for kicks."

Young men can be easily influenced to cross the line between acceptable violence in war and committing atrocities against humanity. Usually, no one tells soldiers to execute innocent civilians or torture victims. Still, a lack of maturity and understanding of the broader implications of their actions can result in deadly and deplorable force. After the fact, if an outcry is large enough, a scapegoat will be found, but in the vast majority of cases, the heinous and brutal acts are largely forgotten in the annals of war.

We see how absurd it is to send boys to war in the documentary *They Shall Not Grow Old.* On the day World War I broke out, young male British rugby players were competing with players from Germany. The next day Germany became their enemy, but many British players believed it was just a game, which excited many teenagers to join up. Even a 14-year-old showed up at Chelsea Barracks hoping to secure his place. He claimed he was 18 and was accepted. "I told them I was 18, and that was it." They were just kids who were naïve and excited. Some aged 15 and 16 tried their luck and were successful. Some aged 17 said they were 19 with their innocent smiling faces like kids, all excited. They were never told where to go and never wondered, "Would I ever come back?" It probably never occurred to the teens in the film that joining the other lads in a spirited competition, played on a battlefield instead of a rugby pitch, would possibly end in death.

Stress and Development

The prefrontal cortex's underdevelopment is especially significant in relation to suicide among young recruits. This bears emphasis on a problem with emotional regulation, executive functioning, and a progression of development which extends into late adolescence and beyond. Exposure to stress can disrupt emotional modulation or inhibitory control and lead to impulsivity and diminished self-control, especially for this age group of recruits with prefrontal cortex deficits. Thus, family stressors, histories of child abuse, marital crises, and multiple combat assignments may be the perfect storm for these vulnerable service members.

A perfect storm is illustrated with an example. A 24-year-old female, JP, was admitted to a field hospital with a mood disorder, having been treated for anxiety. She had received numerous LORs (letters of reprimand) and LOCs (letters of counseling) during her one year of military service. Her most recent misstep was that she had threatened to injure her supervisor by stabbing him in the eye, because she felt her supervisor held a personal grudge against her. JP was convinced that the supervisor's demeanor mirrored that of her mother. Her history of early childhood abuse trauma by her mother had been torturous at times. At age nine, she and her brother would frequently receive beatings at night from their mom after using the bathroom. The floor was in disrepair, and their footsteps would cause a creaking sound, which caused their mother to lose it.

JP was exposed to even worse violence when she saw her mother try to shoot her dad. In another instance, she witnessed her dad violently grab her mother and stuff her in a garbage container. Following her parents' separation, CPS investigated the abusive behavior, and she and her brother were removed from the home. The court awarded custody solely to her father. Unfortunately, JP never bonded with either parent.

Maladapted people often find their way into the service as an attractive alternative to their problems at home, school, or work. Through appropriate mentoring and professional help, some can be successful. Untreated severe psychopathology, however, has its ugly side. It may surface at unfortunate moments and present a formidable challenge that is too difficult for the military service and the recruit to overcome. In my opinion, JP should never have been allowed anywhere near a field of battle in the first place.

★★★

As an experienced psychiatrist I believe there is good evidence for the argument that teenagers should not be allowed in active war zones. I'll provide several case studies in this chapter that provide food for thought in relation to that argument. There is also undoubtedly a counterargument that, of the hundreds of thousands of young men and women under the age of 20 who have served in the U.S. military, many of them have gone on to have productive careers and lives.

For many 18-year-olds who aspire to serve, joining the military or serving in a time of war can mark a successful transition from adolescence into adulthood. Military service offers a great opportunity to experience this "rite of passage," providing a "green card" to freedom and maturity. By establishing oneself as a successful and respectable soldier, the experience, in perpetuity, means they are accepted into adulthood. However, to be young and immature, not ready for some of life's most serious challenges, often places youth at a crossroads where experience is a harsh teacher. She gives the test before the lesson. Some examples of 20-year-olds from my service experience illustrate these problems. As one Air Force veteran, Jeff Bamberg, who served as Captain in the USAF for seven years, eloquently phrased it, "The challenges of having 18-to-25-year-old testosterone bags full of muscle is that they still have the impulse control of 18-to-25-year-old testosterone bags full of muscle!"

However, such stories do not necessarily indicate that every young soldier has the same issues. The fact that there are so many individuals unfit for service bears scrutiny. Age is but one factor; mental health and family history ought to be considered but generally are not. Even one misfit in a company can cause catastrophic consequences

Damaged Goods

During my reserve time in the U.S. Army, when I was not on active duty, I would work at a large military medical center as a full-time Department of Defense psychiatrist with the Department of Behavioral Health. Patients from all branches of the service were referred to me through the chain of command (most of the time via a 1st sergeant or their commanding officer). There were others who would initiate a (voluntary) referral. Reasons for a mental health referral varied and would depend on the severity of their emotional distress. Following my evaluation, some might require immediate hospitalization. Suicide notes would always raise a red flag with the chain of command. Many of these soldier patients and other service members had experienced combat trauma and were air-vac'd out of theater (Iraq/Afghanistan) to the U.S. Army field hospital in Germany before being flown to the states. The following are examples from my case load of patients during my active duty and reserve (civilian officer, army) time. Fitness for duty was always a priority of interest for the military and depending on the severity and complexity of their depression, anxiety, or post-traumatic stress I would determine whether fitness for duty was a temporary or a permanent issue. In some selective cases my disposition would be to discharge them from military service and refer them for follow-up care via one of the VA medical centers.

In 2006, after five months of volunteering at a NATO mass casualty hospital, a young soldier, JJ, was returning from deployment to Kandahar. He joined at age 20 and volunteered in less than a year into his deployment. During half of his time in deployment, he was assigned to a hospital as the first responder to casualties at an airfield. He had worked the night shifts and saw incredible trauma. He became the number one speed dial for extracting helicopter victims. He witnessed horrific carnage daily and had no time to reflect until he returned to the States.

Most troubling, he told me, "A guy with his face blown off, I had to carry a leg, just a leg. I couldn't tell whose part it had come from. I had my hand into someone's chest."

His main complaint was, "I'm always nervous." He tapped his feet in tremor-like motion with urgency and a look of anxiousness and fear. He spoke of his homecoming to Christmas as "overwhelming." He described many dreams: "They bring me back; I get put in all kinds of scenarios." On a recent domestic flight, as he gazed around at other passengers in the plane, "His face went to blood, shrapnel, and charred remains." He complained of experiencing paranoia in the dark at home when he went to bed, looked out the window, and said he was always on guard. His symptoms of PTSD would continue for more than a decade, an unrelenting reminder of what happens when someone is helplessly ill-prepared to meet an emotionally charged situation.

The following cases are from a field hospital. Another soldier, RC, was, by then, in his early twenties, after having entered the Iraq war at 19, only six-to-nine months after joining the army. His chief complaint was, "I still have anger, nightmares, and I can't stand cannon gunfire. I don't think I could deploy again." He continued to be easily triggered by reminders of combat in Iraq. In one reported incident during field training, he became so angry that he blacked out, pushed a vehicle, and ripped off his body armor. I recommended that he receive an honorable discharge and ongoing treatment through the VA hospital system stateside.

An even more tragic illustration is that of a 22-year-old enlistee, CL, who thought he was more intelligent than everyone else. "I'll show you," he said to his commanding officer. After receiving an Article 15 punishment (usually, one's rank, respect, and dignity are lost), he became clinically depressed. The airman sent lengthy suicide notes to his supervisor and eventually killed himself with a shotgun.

JJ, RC, and CL were all seriously unfit to serve in a war zone, each for different reasons, but with similar outcomes. Once they entered service, they became problems to solve, consumed valuable resources, caused some trouble for other soldiers, and ultimately devastated their own lives. Were they too young to join? Age was probably one factor but not the only one. If these individuals had joined the service but were kept away from war zones, they might have still been problematic, though less so, with the stakes significantly reduced.

Sometimes teenagers have performed extraordinary acts of courage and bravery on battlefields, but that doesn't mean they don't become "damaged goods." Consider the World War II Medal of Honor winner Audie Murphy. At age 19, he courageously held off the German soldiers at Colmar but paid a hefty price. Murphy struggled for years with memories of the war and was frequently suicidal, suffering from isolation and nightmares. Author David Morris (*The Evil Hours*) tells of his struggle even 10 years after Murphy returned from the war, when he began sleeping alone in his garage to be farther away from the noises of the house. He quotes Murphy: "In combat, you see, your hearing gets so acute you can interpret any noise. But now, there were all kinds of noises that I couldn't interpret" (Morris, 2015). Additionally, the six U.S. Marines ranging in age from 18 to 23 who courageously raised the American flag on Mt. Suribachi, capturing national attention, and raising the morale of millions of Americans at home, were not spared the struggle with the trauma of war and suffered from post-traumatic stress and physical disabilities, deeply impacted by their wartime experiences. They carried the weight of their sacrifices for the rest of their lives.

Another scarred individual from World War II was the writer J. D. Salinger. The author of *Catcher in the Rye* presents an excellent example of how soldiers are scarred whether or not they fight on a battlefield.

Salinger joined when he was 23 and served as a counterintelligence agent in the 12th Infantry with five campaigns in the European Theater in 1944–45, beginning with the Normandy invasion and ending with the Battle of Hürtgen Forest, which killed or wounded 33,000 U.S. soldiers. He was a World War II combat survivor who struggled with the emotional scars of war trauma. Authors David Shields and Shane Salerno write in the biography, *Salinger*:

> He is a recluse in as much as the last half of his life, avoiding the public, hiding from the media, obscure and unrelenting to the joy of the fruits of fame or notoriety … but I believe with him, as with other traumatized combat vets— delayed PTSD symptoms of survivor's guilt haunt them like a demonic force. For Salinger, he no doubt carried the wounds of his dead comrades within his soul, a pain which no amount of writer glory could expel (Shields and Salerno, 2013).

Many soldiers who also served during times of war but were spared from serving in a war zone similarly suffered from survivor's guilt. Indeed, serving in the military but not being in an active war zone can lead to serious psychological issues for certain individuals with maladaptive coping mechanisms. Whether they were 18 or 35 would probably not matter. In truth, they were probably unfit to serve in any capacity and at any age. Issues don't show up until the soldier complains or his commanding officer reports a problem. The inner turmoil such people suffer may go undiagnosed for days, months, or even years.

While some individuals will suffer at any age, and wherever they are sent, being younger and being in a war zone puts soldiers at more risk of both physical and mental harm.

Lost Souls in Over Their Heads and WOOTS (Want Out of The Service)

What follows are clinical cases from a U.S. Army field hospital. These active-duty service members, for various reasons, required mental health intervention. Such problems as naivety of military expectation combined with peer pressure or intolerance to the mandated demands of military duties, loss of a family member—became a burden too stressful to bear in the context of unresolved childhood psychopathology, maladaptive and self-defeating coping strategies, and immaturity. CC was 22 when he presented to the clinic feeling nervous and anxious because he was far from his family, although he could email or call them daily. He said he joined on a whim along with two of his peers. He never had any idea that he might be subjected to deployment. He said he was doing okay at work and with his supervisor but wanted to get out of the military. Upon further questioning, he admitted that he knew the primary purpose of the military was for the defense of the country. Still, it never occurred to him that his life would be in jeopardy until he was deployed near an active battle zone. And why would he? His life up until that point had always been defined by safety and guardrails. It's one thing to understand what soldiers do in battle; it's quite another to witness firsthand one's peers, equally emotionally unprepared, breaking down under relentless pressure.

Another enlistee, Boe, who joined at age 21, was brought in by his first sergeant, who was concerned about the slash over his left wrist. Although he stated that it was "just being in the wrong place at the wrong time," the sergeant was suspicious. And for a good reason. It turned out that the cut was concurrent with the death of the young man's father. He had carried the entire weight of responsibility of caring for his father in his last days. He was also a power of attorney. Further questioning revealed that he'd had a difficult childhood and would self-harm to relieve stress.

The chain of command became involved with a 20-year-old airman, Sal, who had overdosed on sleeping pills, "I wanted to go to sleep and never wake up," she told me. She stated that she dreaded going to work every day. Had she ever been depressed or suicidal before joining the military? Far from it. By all accounts, up until she enlisted, she had no history of depression, no thoughts of suicide, and appeared to be well suited for service.

Danny, age 76, recalls, as a young Army medic, when he encountered a 17-year-old, Jerry, during his performance of physical examinations on enlistees who had volunteered to be deployed to Vietnam in 1965. "I saw him tearing up, and I asked what's wrong. He replied, 'I don't want to go.'" Danny queried, "Then why did you sign up?" Jimmy replied, "Because all of my entire company volunteered, I couldn't let them down." He actually wasn't suited but was swayed by peers. Looking back to that time, Danny reflects, "I failed him, so he couldn't go. It saved his life; I have no regrets."

Like so many other young men who have gone off to war, some volunteer due to peer pressure, patriotism, and conviction to a cause they embrace or at least think it is the "right thing to do." Others are "striving to achieve manhood" or a "rite of passage." During the Vietnam War, 30 percent of the fighting force were between 18 and 19, many of whom had never graduated from high school.

A 20-year-old, TJ, with two years of time in service (TIS), joined at age 18. He was admitted to a field hospital following his deployment to Iraq. He had texted, "I'm going to kill myself." He took an overdose of medication, an antidepressant he was prescribed, but when I talked with him, he still wanted to remain in the service and evidenced no symptoms of PTSD. TJ refused to elaborate on his history of numerous hospitalizations, but I learned he was married. He did not want to share information about his wife or her problems. TJ's medical history and sudden weight loss of 20 pounds raised concerns that he was unfit to return to a combat situation. A recommendation was given for reassignment to support if he wanted to stay in the service.

Another serviceman, JR, came to see me with a T-3 profile (restrictions for carrying a weapon), which meant that the Army had already deemed him at least temporarily unfit for active-duty service. He was 23, having joined at age 21, unhappy and a WOOTS. On his medical profile, he complained of chronic pain and self-reported depression for the past two years. He stated if his command would not discharge him, "I will go AWOL." He later admitted to homicidal ideation with a systemized plan toward his company commanding officer.

Another WOOTS, PJ, age 20 at the time of his enlistment, never deployed. "I just hate being in the military," he said. He was admitted for psychiatric treatment for telling his friend, "I don't feel like going on." His command planned to chapter him out, "and then they told me they denied it for some reason, so I just lost all hope to get out."

His unit planned to be deployed to Iraq in April 2007, one month after his hospital admission. PJ revealed his strongest impulse to join the Army: "it was part of the hype and what the recruiters told me that prompted me to join." Before his hospital stay, he was AWOL for one month. "I just had to get out of here. I was tired of being in the military and had to get away from it… Every day, I wake up and feel like I want to explode, but I can't."

He had managed to get through basic with some difficulties. He believed that his NCO didn't like him, and he related that his suicidal ideation began when he returned from AWOL. He then resorted to self-mutilation, admitting "I hit myself in the face," as a coping mechanism for stress reduction. His background information supported the premise of having been raised in a stable family environment by both biological parents, who were nurturing, caring, and good-natured. Although an only child, he never felt lonely during his developmental years. He enjoyed friends who frequented his house and did well at school. Sometime after high school graduation, his friends who had already joined the military influenced him to follow their passion.

Yet another example was 18-year-old MP who was admitted to the hospital for thoughts of suicide. "It's been building up from dealing with people at work," he said. He had no psychopathology history and good parental bonding and support. "I just want to be released from the Air Force. I can't stand it anymore," he said. MP had one and a half years in the service. He had joined at age 17 before he became "just a little depressed." His plans changed after entering the military, and he became far more interested in returning home to work at his family business.

Addiction and Dysfunctional Families

Sometimes enlistees turn to alcohol as their main coping mechanism, as exemplified by 18-year-old SY, who found herself struggling with a drinking problem shortly after joining. Though she was too young to purchase alcohol in the United States legally, she found easy access to beer, wine, and hard liquor in the Army. After failing alcohol rehabilitation, she was told she would be separated from the service. However, she was intent on staying. In a hopeless and desperate emotional state, she hooked a hose to an exhaust pipe in a futile attempt to asphyxiate herself and was discovered by the police. Her suicide attempt was prompted when she heard her commander state that her unit was departing to sea aboard a Navy ship. She also had been recently hospitalized at another facility for supposedly cutting her wrists. When in the Army, those who are marginally fit and struggling to cope with stress, may resort to negative ways to manage their situation, including alcohol and in extreme cases, weapons.

All too often, I saw youth who joined the service and who had come from a troubled or abusive family or childhood. The lack of stability in their lives before entering the service made them completely unprepared for the rigors of military life. They washed out, unable to deal with the mandates, pressures, and stress of military life. But it wasn't just those with tough upbringings who became depressed and suicidal. I witnessed young enlistees aged 18 or 19 from good nurturing families and with no history of child psychopathology, who many times were not at the appropriate maturational age to successfully fulfill their military obligation. The issue is that it's not one-size-fits-all in the game of age and recruitment. There are more men than women in the military, and many young men lack maturity. Some essential brain tracks are not laid down until men reach their 20s.

Studies by pediatricians and developmental psychologists have concluded that throughout the developmental years from kindergarten (age five) to age 12, girls on average have a one-to-two-year advantage in social and emotional maturity over boys of the same age. Often, the young and naïve are drawn to military service but their immaturity places them in a vulnerable position.

Military life can present difficult and insurmountable hurdles for teens going through a period of impulsivity and confusion in their search for identity. Those who have not succeeded in their adolescent journey may find even greater identity crises in military service. However, for those who are fortunate enough to find a helpful mentor who they can trust, they have a much greater chance to succeed.

The status quo of sending teenagers into combat zones is clearly not working, as evidenced by the mental health statistics (a seven times greater chance to develop PTSD (Dohrenwend et al., 2013) and case studies I described. Something needs to change to better protect our youth from trauma while also strengthening our military. Who will make the difficult choices, and how will decisions affecting the lives of millions of people be made?

In essence, we need to have a more open, honest dialogue about the realities of military service for youth and implement wise reforms that protect them from trauma while also strengthening our armed forces. With the right policies and leadership practices in place, we can achieve the noble goal of improving military readiness responsibly and ethically.

CHAPTER 4

Why Do Teenagers Enlist?

Military recruiters have an enormous responsibility, yet too often, they exploit the young and innocent with lofty promises and appeals to patriotism. Their mandate is to meet monthly quotas, which creates pressure to sign up candidates regardless of their fitness for service. They, unfortunately, exploit the young and innocent with many promises, such as becoming part of something bigger than themselves or transforming their lives. Without the draft, of course, it's a free-for-all. Army recruiters have a mandate—a minimum of three new recruits per month. This quota puts them under pressure to ensure their promotions and 20-year pensions are secured. In many cases, the system has lowered the standards; for example, recruiters have no problem signing up those who have had felony offenses, or a judge could waive a one-year prison sentence and allow the accused to join the military instead. In other cases, a string of psychiatric hospitalizations for suicide attempts was not discovered as a disqualifier. This "quantity over quality" approach leads to many tragic outcomes that could be avoided with proper screening.

Perhaps the worst deceit comes through glossy marketing campaigns targeting impressionable youth. Slick ads promise potential recruits that they can "be all you can be" and that the military will "make you strong." These empty platitudes prey on teens' insecurities and desire for purpose, adventure, and belonging. Recruiters also rely heavily on peer pressure, exhorting youth to enlist alongside their friends. Once training begins, there is no easy way out.

Greater oversight and reform of recruitment practices are sorely needed. We must have an open and honest dialogue with youth about the psychological demands of military service before they sign up. If we are sending teenagers into harm's way to potentially lose their lives, we owe them the best preparation and care from the very start. Anything less is unethical.

There may not be a perfectly suitable age for all to begin their service duty, yet I have seen too many who served in a war zone suffer psychological damage for the rest of their lives. The lingering burden of chronic survivor's guilt has many variations of pain and moments of intense darkness, leaving the surviving soldier thoughtless and stoic. As Harold Moore and Joseph Galloway, authors of *We Were Soldiers Once ... And Young*, stated, "It's easy to forget the numbers, but how can we forget the faces, the voices, the cries of young men dying before their time?"

War happens in seconds, but the memories are recalled forever. Some who are haunted by memories say their face gets hot, and blood is suddenly loud in their ears. That triad often spoken by psychologists is "fight, flight, or freeze." As David Morris, author of *The Evil Hours*, writes, "One of the odd paradoxes of trauma is that it happens in a moment, but it can consume a lifetime... The daemonic night and its chief product, the nightmare, have always been a special hell for survivors."

Military Service as a Route to College

For many individuals, adolescence is incomplete at age 18 or 19. For them, the choice is often between enrollment in college or enlistment in the military. It has been stated that the U.S. military screens out virtually no one except for an apparent medical defect. I experienced this myself when I tried to join in my early 20s but was rejected because of a football injury I sustained.

Those who cannot afford horrifically expensive college tuition believe the military offers them a clear path to education without debt. And so, it does. But those who volunteer for service to gain a college diploma don't necessarily make the best soldiers. I can't blame those who decide to join at age 18 or 19 because they can't afford to go to college;

I understand that they are making hard decisions at a time in their life when they have few viable choices.

While some young recruits adapt well to military life, many lack the maturity and psychological readiness at 18 to handle the immense stresses of service, especially in combat zones. More rigorous screening based on mental health, family background, and motivations could help identify those unfit for service. For youth seeking education, incentives besides military enrollment may better prepare them as citizens. With policy changes, we can minimize tragedies among the young while still maintaining a solid defense.

The hard choices facing policymakers should not be made in a vacuum or by people who do not understand what it means to serve our country. Captain Ben Catlin, who attended the Air Force Academy and served in the USAF for nearly seven years, told a poignant story that highlights this point:

> I was at a Naval Academy Foreign Affairs conference which was one of the high-level military-oriented conferences. And I was sitting there with a guy from Harvard, a guy from Yale, and a guy from Princeton. I think between them, they might have read 12 or 13 articles about the military. And I thought, I'm just gonna sit here and see how long it takes for them to actually ask me a question. And after half an hour, I finally got annoyed, and I said, "You know, the topic you're talking about is 100 percent oriented toward real military experience. I'm third generation military. None of you guys have any idea what you're talking about." It taught me a valuable lesson for life, which is that an awful lot of people who go into government have absolutely no idea what to do with the military, but somehow, they think they do because they're smart and have academic backgrounds.

Existing research has uncovered several perspectives on the effectiveness of military education benefits, particularly the Post-9/11 GI Bill, regarded as the most comprehensive education benefits package offered to eligible military personnel (Glass-Coffin, 2019). For example, according to Skomsvold, Radford, and Berkner (2011), military education benefits positively impact degree attainment among veterans, regardless of their socioeconomic background. Similarly, Rudd et al. (2011) found that accessing military education benefits increased veterans' persistence in completing their college education.

However, veterans' academic success in military education benefits programs is not universal. For example, Bogue (2013) highlighted that veterans often face obstacles when transitioning from military life to a college environment, including difficulties adjusting to civilian norms and mental health challenges. Furthermore, some educational institutions have been accused of exploiting military educational benefits programs by enrolling veterans in low-quality programs, with these students often dropping out without attaining a degree (Shefrick, 2018).

Despite these challenges, military education benefits have overwhelmingly had a positive impact on career prospects. For example, Barr (2018) found that veterans using the Post-9/11 GI Bill had a higher likelihood of employment in their career field and increased earning potential than those who did not use their benefits. This finding suggests that the government's investment in military education benefits may yield long-term returns in employment and workforce development and certainly on a personal level for those veterans who have excelled and found a demand not only for their degree but for training and experience. Moreover, various corporations have recently recognized and coveted these attributes in their hiring practices.

To make the policy even more effective, the government could and should invest in better support services for veterans, such as mental health care, career counseling, health service specialties, and specific training programs tailored to their needs and the market's incentives. Such initiatives should be a central part of the program and provide academic counseling to those active-duty service members, especially those unsure of their choice of an academic curriculum or a major. As a therapist, I believe counseling should be done well before discharge to give veterans the greatest chance of post-military service success.

In my opinion, the military's guarantee of a college degree is a worthwhile and effective government policy. The benefits extend beyond savings on tuition costs, providing young people with an alternative pathway to higher education and a foundation for a stable and rewarding career.

In 1932, less than 5 percent of qualified individuals went to college, but by 1964 that number climbed to 60 percent. It's fair to say that the GI Bill of Rights, which guaranteed veterans a college education, transformed the United States. Becoming a college graduate went from a rarity to a societal norm. College didn't necessarily make Americans more intelligent, but it exposed them to new ideas and cultures.

Military Service as a Stepping-stone to Success

Jimi Hendrix, an iconic musician widely considered one of the greatest guitarists in history, lived amid a rapidly changing social and political climate. Born into poverty in Seattle, Washington, in 1942, Hendrix faced a turbulent childhood marked by family turmoil and frequent relocations. Despite these challenges, he developed a passion for music and began playing the guitar at 15. As a self-taught musician, Hendrix drew inspiration from diverse sources such as blues, jazz, and rock and roll (Cross, 2010).

In the early 1960s, Hendrix's career gained momentum as he played with several bands, including the Isley Brothers and Little Richard's band. In 1966, he formed the Jimi Hendrix Experience, which quickly gained popularity in the UK and later in the U.S. Hendrix's innovative guitar playing and electrifying performances made him a sensation in the music world and a symbol of the 1960s counterculture movement. His influence on music endures today, and his legacy as a pioneering musician and cultural icon remains firmly intact.

Hendrix's decision to join the U.S. Army in 1961 continues to spark debate among scholars, music enthusiasts, and fans. Some argue he enlisted to avoid jail time for car theft, while others believe he was genuinely interested in serving his country. Given his background and upbringing, college was likely never a serious consideration. He probably joined to avoid a potential jail sentence (Cross, 2010).

Despite his difficult childhood, marked by poverty, neglect, and abuse, Hendrix found solace in music. By his teenage years, he was already playing in local bands. However, he was forced to choose between jail time or the Army after legal troubles caught up with him. Hendrix chose the latter and was deployed to Fort Campbell, Kentucky. While in the Army, he continued to play music, forming a band with fellow soldiers.

Yet Hendrix found military life stifling and longed for civilian life. His time in the Army later influenced his music, as he often incorporated military imagery and themes in his songs.

During his Army service, Hendrix formed a close friendship with a fellow soldier and bassist, Billy Cox. The two met while stationed at Fort Campbell and bonded over their shared love of music. As a result, they formed a band called The King Kasuals, which played gigs at local clubs and venues around the base. This friendship was a lasting one, as Cox would later join Hendrix's post-Experience band, the short-lived but influential Band of Gypsies. Despite Hendrix's later less-than-positive comments about his time in the U.S. Army, his military service instilled discipline and a strong work ethic, which he maintained throughout his career.

A recent article by J. P. Morgan (February 18, 2022) argues that former military service members make ideal entrepreneurs with key qualities which transfer to the business world. "They are driven, calm under pressure and expert problem solvers." Another reason why military veterans thrive in professional settings is their strong work ethic and sense of discipline. During their service they are instilled with a deep commitment to their duties and responsibilities. They understand the importance of hard work, dedication, and going above and beyond the call of duty. This work ethic makes them highly reliable and capable of meeting tight deadlines and exceeding expectations in their respective professional roles.

A notable example is Bob Parsons, the founder of GoDaddy. Parsons served as a rifleman in the Marine Corps during the Vietnam War. His military experience instilled in him the determination and resilience necessary to build a successful business empire.

Another veteran, Howard Schultz, former CEO of Starbucks, served in the U.S. Army before growing the iconic coffee company and turning it into a global powerhouse. Moreover, David Oreck, the founder of Oreck Corporation, is a prime example of how military training can translate into success. Oreck's experience in the Air Corps during World War II informed his business approach, leading to the development of the popular Oreck vacuum cleaners.

Former Navy SEAL Chris Taylor, co-founder of Mission Essential (a cybersecurity company) acquired from his military experience a strategic mindset of attention to detail. This skill transferred as an asset to his success in a complex and rapidly evolving world of cybersecurity. These examples merely scratch the surface of countless former veterans who have made their mark in the civilian business and professional world.

Hendrix is but one of many who were lost as adolescents but benefited from lessons learned through military service—some who opted for service as a means to a college education, some to escape difficult family dynamics, and others because they had no better options at the time. Notable examples include Audie Murphy, one of World War II's most decorated American combat soldiers. Growing up in a low-income family in Texas, he faced a challenging childhood before enlisting in the military at 17. His military service led to significant achievements, including receiving the Medal of Honor for his actions in battle. After the war, Murphy became a successful actor, starring in over 40 films and penning his memoir, *To Hell and Back*.

Before becoming a renowned singer-songwriter and actor, Kris Kristofferson served in the U.S. Army as a helicopter pilot. He achieved the rank of captain and served in West Germany during the early 1960s. After leaving the military, Kristofferson pursued a successful career in music and acting, with hits such as "Me and Bobby McGee" and roles in films like *A Star Is Born*. Ironically, and unlike most people who join a branch of the armed services, before he began his military service in the early 1960s, Kristofferson had already received his bachelor's degree from Pomona College and studied at Oxford University as a Rhodes Scholar in 1958.

Many other famous actors and performers served in the military. They later used their benefits to attend college, including Clint Eastwood, who served in the Korean War and then studied business administration at Los Angeles City College, and Gene Hackman, who was a radio operator in the U.S. Marine Corps, following which he attended the University of Illinois. Other distinguished veterans who benefited from the GI Bill include Morgan Freeman, James Earl Jones, Alan Alda, Bea Arthur, and Pat Sajak.

On average, most service members complete at least one term of enlistment (four to six years) before deciding whether to continue serving or transition to civilian life. Others make a career out of their military service, putting in 20 years and then retiring to the private sector, where their skills are in high demand. An example is Jocko Willink, a former Navy SEAL officer who became a successful entrepreneur and author after his 20-year military career. Willink grew up without much direction and failed out of college twice. He eventually became a Navy SEAL officer and served in various leadership positions. After leaving the Navy, Willink co-founded a leadership consulting firm and authored several books on leadership including *Extreme Ownership*.

These individuals are just a few examples of people who have used their military service to overcome personal struggles, develop discipline and focus, and ultimately succeed in various fields. Some used the GI military education benefit to enroll in college, while others decided to forego the benefit. Either way, the military is often an excellent option for those undecided about a career choice. In addition, having the option of a full-ride scholarship empowers many young people who would otherwise have no chance to attain higher education.

The original GI Bill, also known as the Servicemen's Readjustment Act of 1944, helped World War II veterans transition to civilian life by providing financial assistance for education, home loans, and unemploy-ment benefits. The most recent version, called the Post-9/11 GI Bill, is even more generous. The new version covers tuition and fees, a monthly housing allowance, and a yearly stipend for books and supplies, and can be used for college degrees, vocational training, and even on-the-job training. Indeed, it endures as one of the most outstanding benefits the United States government offers. Since 2009, more than 2.3 million veterans have used the Post-9/11 GI Bill for education.

Remarkably, military service has the potential to propel individuals from struggle to success. Michael Freeman's book, *From Failing Hands to Fighting Chance: How Military Service Changed My Life*, is a testament to this fact. Freeman shares his story of growing up in poverty and battling addiction before enlisting in the Navy. Military service provided him with structure, discipline, and camaraderie, enabling him to overcome personal struggles and become a successful business owner. Many veterans, like Freeman, credit their military service with equipping them with the tools and skills necessary for success in civilian life. Despite the challenges and risks of military service, the potential for personal growth and success is indisputable.

In the United States, military experience has always been highly valued, with transitioning from military to civilian life considered a crucial step in a veteran's journey. This experience has created a new path for career advancement through military service (Schulmeister, 2021). In addition, military experience can help veterans develop various sought-after skills in the civilian job market, such as leadership, teamwork, problem-solving, and adaptability. This development has opened up new opportunities for veterans seeking career advancement or transitioning into a new field.

Perhaps the most illustrative example among those individuals who leveraged a military career to triumph over impoverishment and discrimination is the late retired General Colin Powell. Powell grew up in a low-income family in the Bronx, New York, and could not afford college. As a result, the military became his "springboard" for achievements beyond his imagination. He joined the ROTC program in college, leading to his commission as a second lieutenant in the U.S. Army. Powell continued to serve in various leadership positions, ultimately achieving the rank of four-star general and becoming the first Black person to serve as the Joint Chiefs of Staff Chairman.

While military service may not be the right option for everyone, it is a path that many have chosen, not only those who could not afford college but also those unsure of their career aspirations. In addition, it has provided an opportunity for tens of thousands of individuals who needed a time interval for maturation and character formation. Subsequently, many of them would eventually enter college, technical school, or an apprenticeship and pursue a successful career.

Recently, apprenticeship training and experience in specialized skill areas of great demand, have attracted young people. This track offers a prosperous alternative to an academic degree which would burden them with significant debt and, in many cases, no guarantee of a job that would match the income of a highly trained skilled worker. Many of these young people seek a career—such as electrician, plumber, or welder—where they can enter the workforce and compete with starting salaries equal to those who have earned a bachelor's degree. Conversely, this becomes a significant competition for military recruitment. Instead, they opt for a skilled career requiring two or fewer years of training and, in some cases, concurrently with a stipend.

Many Fortune 500 companies have also long recognized the value of hiring veterans, leading to the establishment of veteran hiring initiatives. For example, Microsoft launched a military affairs office to help veterans find employment. Other corporations prioritizing hiring veterans include Amazon, Lockheed Martin, Northrop Grumman, Boeing, GE, Verizon, JP Morgan Chase, and Walmart. Despite those who disparage every aspect of military service, it's clear that military experience is a valuable asset in today's job market, and veterans should seize the available opportunities to advance their careers.

The military attracts many people who join because they can't think of anything else to do with their lives. They wander through adolescence and early adulthood with no direction and hope that joining the military will provide leadership and guidance. Unfortunately, many such individuals have no idea what they are getting into until it's too late, especially for those with maladaptive coping mechanisms.

Quantifying the Psychological Benefits of Service

Military service has historically catalyzed transformation and led to personal growth for hundreds of thousands. Those who have served recount how their experiences have significantly benefited various aspects of their lives, from overcoming adversity and achieving success to discovering new career paths. Without question, although it is not for everyone, military service has proven to be a life-changing opportunity for countless people.

Perhaps the main reason military service has proven beneficial is that service demands individuals confront adversity and foster personal growth (Hawkins, 2016). Service also offers a unique platform for developing resilience, self-discipline, and leadership skills, all crucial for personal development. Soldiers experience demanding situations but learn how to manage stress, regulate emotions, and cultivate a sense of purpose and meaning. Furthermore, military service fosters camaraderie, belonging, and a shared sense of purpose, promoting personal growth and a sense of community. Despite the inherent challenges and difficulties, soldiers who overcome adversity and grow personally often report increased life satisfaction and a sense of achievement.

While military service entails substantial stress and sacrifice, an emerging body of research demonstrates it can also strengthen mental health in multiple dimensions when approached as a personal growth experience. Rigorous studies have begun quantifying how service cultivates resilience, purpose, self-esteem, and other psychological traits that enhance well-being and functioning long-term. However, some studies report data contrary to this when the impact of psychological stress, for those who served in combat, is weighed in.

A resilience in veterans study (Thomas et al., 2017) of 1,480 U.S. veterans in a national representative survey revealed that combat veterans were three times as likely to screen positive for lifetime PTSD and had a 82 percent greater odds of screening positive for generalized anxiety disorder than non-combat veterans.

Conversely another intriguing study compared mental health outcomes between Israeli veterans of elite combat units and non-combat reservists (Greene et al., 2020). While both groups experienced wartime trauma, the elite unit veterans reported higher levels of post-traumatic growth, defined as positive psychological changes after trauma, such as deepened relationships or new possibilities. This research suggests the intense bonding and meaning derived from elite service buffered against trauma's harmful mental health effects.

Beyond purpose and growth, military service has also been linked to boosted resilience: the ability to navigate adversity and stress without lasting dysfunction. For example, a 2019 meta-analysis synthesized results across 16 studies on resilience in active-duty service members and veterans (Leppin et al., 2014). It confirmed military populations exhibited significantly higher resilience levels than the general public. Service members' rigorously developed coping skills, self-efficacy, and ability to tolerate discomfort accounted for their greater resilience capacity.

Relatedly, a longitudinal study by Elder and Clipp (1989) tracked the life trajectories of World War II veterans. It found 60 percent believed their experience made them more self-confident and decisive when facing future challenges, enhancing resilience. Only 4 percent felt military service made them less assured and capable. This result aligns with studies showing veterans maintain better psychological health during crises like the COVID-19 pandemic relative to civilians (Perales et al., 2021).

Military service has also been associated with improved self-esteem and confidence, though effects differ across demographic groups. For instance, in a pioneering 1972 study, Vietnam veterans were surveyed on their self-esteem post-service (Egendorf et al., 1981). Most reported higher self-esteem after returning home and transitioning to civilian life compared to when they began service. However, African American veterans saw diminishing gains, likely due to facing prejudice both in the military and after.

In the landmark National Vietnam Veterans Readjustment Study, over 1,600 veterans were assessed 20 years after their service (Frueh et al., 2004) The majority reported struggling with issues like depression and feeling alienated from society. But positive self-esteem and confidence in social settings were frequently endorsed strengths nurtured through military service. This study highlights the nuanced psychological impact of military service across different eras and populations. Many veterans have experienced the horrors of war firsthand, leading to enduring psychological scars. Everyone has a breaking point, and it is difficult if not impossible to predict which trauma or how much repetitive trauma will be the one which causes a mental collapse, break down. To the military's credit there is now a movement under way to provide resilience training as a prophylactic measure for those ordered to combat duty. Success of such strategies will have to wait for conclusive results for a verification of efficacy.

While these findings illuminate strengths derived from military service, challenges remain. Self-selection factors complicate determining causality, as those drawn to service often possess high baseline resilience. Discrimination and trauma also condition outcomes among marginalized groups. Studies consistently pinpoint enhanced purpose, growth, resilience, and self-esteem as psychological benefits frequently derived from military service.

These positive traits do not emerge automatically. Realizing the mental health benefits of service likely depends on viewing one's experience as an avenue for personal development. Approaching service with a "growth mindset" that frames challenges as opportunities to become stronger and wiser leads to maximal psychological gain. Support from fellow service members is another factor that contributes to one facing and overcoming trauma.

With wise framing and mentoring from leaders and peers, military service can thus incubate profound psychological strengths that enhance well-being long after service concludes. This powerfully affirms military life as not just a job but a transformative journey imparting purpose and lifelong resilience even amid adversity. Quantifying these emerging benefits provides additional motivation for those considering enlistment to join the ranks and embark on their growth journey.

The Arguments for and Against Compulsory Service

Compulsory military service has not existed in the U.S. except during war/conflict. However, in several countries worldwide, conscription has been an essential component of national defense to protect the country from its neighboring countries in the event of hostility and to ensure that the country has a well-functioning military force ready to defend the nation. Military conscription can also help to develop a sense of shared sacrifice and significantly impact social integration. Countries like Germany, Greece, Russia, and China have compulsory military service policies. In these countries, required military service can range from several months to years. By comparison, compulsory military service in other countries has not had a significant influence on career decisions as it has had in Israel, for example.

In some countries, conscripts do not receive any significant benefits after leaving the military, and their service may even hinder their career choices or prospects. In Israel, the Israeli Defense Forces (IDF) provides soldiers with skills, training, and experience that prepare them for civilian employment opportunities, particularly for those who may not have had access to higher education. In addition, the IDF has programs that allow soldiers to obtain civilian certifications, such as in nursing, engineering, and computer science.

In the U.S., the recent upsurge in apprenticeships has provided young people with various career opportunities. For instance, in 2017, under the administration of President Trump, an executive order expanded apprenticeships and job training opportunities. Based on the U.S. Department of Labor and Employment data as of 2021, apprenticeship programs have seen a 64 percent increase since 2012.

Apprenticeships provide an opportunity to earn while you learn. Research indicates that the resurgence in apprenticeships has had an impact on military enlistment numbers. In a 2020 article, Bearce found that apprenticeships were among the top career choices for students considering alternatives to military service. The research indicates that more young people consider this a suitable career path. In contrast, others use it as a stepping stone for further education or to gain work experience before joining the military.

Shooting Itself in the Foot: The Recruiting Crisis

In recent years, there has been a noticeable decrease in military recruitment rates, raising concerns about the ability of armed forces to meet their personnel needs. A recent article from the *Tampa Bay Times*, "Here's what's going on with the problem of low military recruitment," (September 30, 2023) cites low unemployment, families advising against it and the shrinking pool of Americans fit to serve. Also noted is a steady decline in enlistment numbers over the past 40 years.

Women's role in the workforce has diversified and many are pursuing civilian careers. Additionally, changing attitudes toward military service has had an impact. Millennials are especially skeptical of the military and its role in society. Some perceive military service as dangerous and unnecessary, particularly in the context of ongoing conflicts in the Middle East and Ukraine. Others view the military as an institution that perpetuates violence and conflict rather than providing a solution to global problems (Asghar, 2017).

In a March 2023 article on the military recruiting crisis, D. Barnes and N. Benshel sound an alarm: "The all-volunteer force may finally have reached its breaking point." Their argument is supported by data—for example, the Army missed its recruiting goal by 15,000 in 2022 and the current fiscal year is likely to be even worse. Among the salient reasons, they write, "For the first time in almost 20 years, American troops are no longer fighting abroad to keep insurgents and terrorists at bay."

A report in the *Military Times* (December 6, 2023), cites the Department of Defense (DOD)'s use of a database known as Genesis, which provides a complete medical history of prospective candidates and flags past and present health problems. As a result, applicants who might have otherwise been able to talk their way in, or obfuscate enough to avoid getting weeded out, are now immediately disqualified. One recruiter noted that of 30 applicants he identified, "only one was clean as a whistle."

The *Military Times* report also noted due to the demanding workload and the complexity of the way the recruitment system has evolved, some recruiters have reportedly engaged in fraudulent activities to enlist recruits more quickly (Castelli, 2018). Tom Bowman, in his August 15, 2006 presentation, "U.S. Military Recruiters Charged with Violations," on National Public Radio, revealed violations ranging from falsifying documents to instructing recruits not to reveal legal or medical problems. More recently, Tori Bateman in her recent article, "Tracking Military Recruiter Abuse," (2023), sounds an alarm stating that "Recruiters encouraged individuals to cheat, lie, or misrepresent themselves in the recruitment process." Such fraudulent practices expose the Army to potential security risks and undermine the institution's credibility. The Law Office of Matthew Barry very recently (January 21, 2024) noted additions to the UCMJ, Article 93a, Army Recruiter Misconduct, which criminalize withholding, altering or concealing applicant information.

As an Army veteran and someone who has treated active-duty soldiers and veterans for more than 30 years, I believe that excessive screening of candidates is detrimental to the overall cause. Should someone be denied the right to serve if they suffered from depression, used marijuana, or broke a bone as a child? Not necessarily—at least in my opinion. In many cases it can depend on other factors as well, e.g., making a healthy adaptation by the child/adolescent given a chance to identify with a compassionate father/mother figure as their mentor. And yet the Genesis medical records database will identify such issues and immediately cause such candidates to be rejected. Overzealous adherence to arbitrary standards is counterproductive and does the U.S. military a disservice. Yes, we want the best, the brightest, the hardest working, the most dedicated, and the most patriotic. It is for this reason that we should consider candidates on a case-by-case basis and not automatically exclude them on a technicality. There are, of course, many extenuating factors that might inform why a candidate is not suitable, whether physical or mental, but it is not a one-size-fits-all model of recruitment.

Another concern recruiters often cite as reasons why they can't find enough candidates is youth obesity rates, which have been, over time, one of the main reasons for military ineligibility. Yes, physical fitness is essential, but someone who is overweight and will never be in a combat role should not be immediately disqualified.

Tom Vanden Brook's story, "The Army is Desperate..." in *USA Today News* (July 5, 2023), highlights the problem of recruitment even further, with fewer recruits being able to pass the Armed Forces Qualification Test (AFQT); in 2022, only 60 percent met that score (31, the minimum overall score for passing). As a result, the Army is preparing to spend more than $100 million to support a fitness school pilot program. Moreover, he emphasizes the awareness of this crisis: "only 23 percent of Americans aged 17 to 24 have academic and physical qualifications to serve." Desperate times call for desperate action, and the draft's popularity went south 50 years ago, at the end of the Vietnam War. Senior journalist Richard Sisk recently stated, "The military recruiting outlook is grim indeed. Loss of public confidence, political attacks and the economy are all taking a toll" (2024). Furthermore, he reveals the confidence in the military declined 20 percentage points in the last 3 years.

It's sad but true that Americans have lost confidence in the military due to recent setbacks and PR issues. The chaotic withdrawal from Afghanistan is cited as another salient reason. Another is the perception of the U.S. military becoming too involved in politics. "Woke" priorities, of great importance to some and irrelevance to others, are seen as undermining the military and causing a drop in the public's confidence.

Focusing too heavily on diversity and inclusion may prioritize identity politics over meritocracy or reward based on race, gender, or personal identity instead of skills, experience, and qualifications (Mahnken et al., 2019).

Maybe such issues only come to the fore during relative peace, when national security is not immediately threatened, so perhaps this is an appropriate time for a healthy dialogue. At the same time, social and societal issues are nearly always divisive and polarizing, making it much harder for the U.S. military to attract qualified candidates. There are no simple answers, but they raise the point that the need for strong leadership has never been more critical. Service members represent the greater population they serve, for better or worse. The strength of the United States has always been the diverse melting pot from which we spring. Actively working to exclude qualified individuals eager to serve can be counterproductive.

A report of the National Independent Panel on Military Service and Readiness (March 30, 2023) released data that reveals a growing politicization where there is an imposition of policies, programs, and messaging not designed for the military but for political reasons.

The panel cited specific concerns; for example, "Including such DEI [Diversity, Equity, Inclusion] training programs impacts not only the public perception of the military but also military culture." With regard to specific training activities, the panel was concerned that being forced to participate in privilege walks which required members to separate themselves by race and gender singled out their perceived privilege.

The military has long been associated with masculine ideals such as physical prowess, aggression, discipline, and stoicism. Historically, these characteristics have been instrumental in shaping the identity of the military and justifying its hierarchical structure (Connell, 1995).

Challenges to those deeply held values, and arguments against a monolithic conception of masculinity, present a challenge for military recruiters who have historically attracted young men/adolescents who aspire to mirror an image of strength, discipline, and leadership and obtain their rite of passage. Military culture has been a mainstay of pride for young people who have had respect for the ethos of mental and physical strength decorum and have set the bar high for training.

However, the shift toward embracing diversity, equity, and inclusion in various sectors of society is becoming increasingly evident. As a critical institution ensuring national security and defense, the military must confront the challenges and ensure that readiness, effectiveness, and merit are not compromised in the changing landscape. There has been an ongoing debate about whether the military should consider factors beyond merit, such as diversity and socioeconomic background when making promotion decisions. Some argue that the military should focus solely on promoting the most qualified candidates based on merit and performance. However, others contend that considering diversity and an individual's personal history can help address historical inequities and discrimination issues within the ranks. They suggest that promoting candidates with different backgrounds and life experiences may benefit the force overall, even if they are not always the top performer on paper. While no official policy states that diversity should be prioritized over merit, there is a discourse about whether attributes aside from qualifications alone should weigh into military promotion systems. While I believe the military should always be a meritocracy, proponents on each side make reasonable arguments. Notwithstanding, no institution in the U.S. is more critical for national defense and freedom than the military, and mission and meritocracy go hand-in-hand.

There are no easy answers, of course. Convincing veterans, active-duty soldiers, and military recruiters that gender issues are important considerations is an uphill battle. Based on my research and personal experience, most people in these groups are unsympathetic because military culture is beginning to change against their will. Indeed, many are openly hostile to such considerations. War is war, and we need tough and resilient fighters; they ask why we are discussing inclusivity and diversity.

Meanwhile, the shortage of recruits has reached a new nadir. In a May 9, 2023 article in *American Military News* titled "Navy suddenly tells retiring troops they owe three more years of service amid recruiting troubles," reporter Kyle Kleeman writes, "At least 65 military doctors and dentists in the Navy Reserves were told on Friday that they still had to undertake at least three more years of service, a shocking development caused by administrative record-keeping errors in their retirement credits, officials claimed as the U.S. military continues to face a historic decline in military recruits." If you can't easily recruit new people, holding on to the ones you have, by whatever means, appears to be a stop-gap measure.

The military, a traditionally apolitical institution, must remain so to continue to be respected by both the elected leaders and the American public. However, the trend of politicization of the military threatens to undermine the institution's credibility and effectiveness. Moreover, a recent report by the Heritage Foundation states that 65 percent of all active-duty service members are very concerned about politics creeping into the military and its ranks.

Young people wanting to choose a career may ponder with some concern whether the military is a reliable option in the long term, with only 17 percent of service members remaining long enough to retire. This percentage may slip further if leadership and direction are not prioritized for credibility and trust.

The military crisis in America must be urgently addressed by the government and military leadership with visionary wisdom. Ensuring the military maintains an apolitical stance and upholds its cherished values is crucial. Officials might do well to recall General MacArthur's 1962 address to the graduates of West Point, in which he said, "the very obsession of your public service must be Duty, Honor, Country."

CHAPTER 5

The Toll of War

They tie up heavy burdens, hard to bear, and lay them on people's shoulders, but they themselves are not willing to move them with their finger.
—MATTHEW 23:4, ENGLISH STANDARD VERSION

Jimmy was born into an intact family in California in the late 1970s. He soon became a product of a fractured family, not unlike many others, and at age 8 his parents split. His mom took him and his 10-year-old brother, his mom's favorite, back to the East Coast. Soon after the divorce, she met an active-duty military fellow and remarried. Without notifying the boys' father, she took them to Germany to live, where her new husband was assigned.

After abruptly losing contact, Jimmy's father became desperate to find his children and was finally able to do so by contacting the Red Cross. He flew to Germany, hired an attorney, and sued for custody. His ex-wife then countersued for sole custody, and the judge awarded custody to both parents with provisions for a six-month stay with each parent every year. It was "fair" but otherwise a bad outcome for everyone. Jimmy would stay with his mom while his brother would be with his father; after six months, they would switch.

When Jimmy was 16, he lived with his grandmother in California until graduation from high school. After that, he would hang out with his dad, who, on Fridays, would smoke pot with his peers. "All we talked about was how awful our life was." He also became acquainted with his cousin (10 years his senior), whom he developed a fondness for, and they shared a mutual bond.

Like his cousin, Jimmy shared an infatuation with the military and joined the Marines when he turned 18 in 1997. Since Jimmy had returned from Germany, he aimed to become an infantry soldier and be at the front. He was anxious to be deployed. This would be his rite of passage, his way to make a statement and become a standout. He had much to prove for his signature of manhood. His military career was his whole life, into which he threw himself with unbridled enthusiasm. It went reasonably well when he initially joined the Marines because Jimmy was so gung-ho, but gradually disenchantment began to creep in.

Before his second deployment to Japan he got married. Upon his return, he had a heart-to-heart talk with his cousin. He told him that he was very disappointed with the military and that they had not followed what they had promised [an infantry assignment]. He never spoke about where he was or what he was doing. In fact, he couldn't because he was in covert operations. Later, it was learned he had been in Iraq helping set up operations for the invasion.

The timing of communication with his cousin was unpredictable. During the Gulf War of 1991, on one occasion he called him from the Philippines, his voice had an urgent tone, "I am in charge, and everybody else is dead!" At that time there was no news that indicated the U.S. military was involved in any combat mission in that country. He always adhered to the military code of secrecy and never disclosed his location for any hostile covert activities. His vitriol came across like a flashback from combat trauma.

After his return from this second deployment, he decided not to reenlist. He wanted to settle down, spend time with his newly-wed wife, and make their life together. The Marines told him, "No, no, no. You've got experience. We can't lose you." They promised not to send him overseas if he would sign. "We need you in the military. America needs you, and we need you for your experience to train those new people coming in."

The appeal to his patriotism didn't win him over so much as the bonds he shared with fellow Marines. So, against his own better judgment, he signed on again. But, only a few days later, he heard the Marines were breaking their promise and deploying him overseas.

The deceit hit him dead center. As angry as he was with the military, he was more furious at himself. How had he allowed himself to be fooled again? In a matter of hours, his life spiraled out of control. Jimmy went to the armory, checked out his rifle, carried it down to a public beach, and shot himself in the head. One might assume that death by suicide might disqualify someone from being honored by the U.S. military, but such is not the case. Jimmy was buried in Arlington National Cemetery.

Although he served with honor and distinction, America's posthumous recognition of his service, to be buried alongside thousands of war heroes, was bittersweet. Should Jimmy have ever been allowed to serve in the Marines? His family believed not. He was, in fact, a ticking timebomb waiting to explode. He did well in a highly disciplined organization but was maladapted to cope with a world outside of a well-defined military role or to speak up against those who sought to take advantage of him. From when he joined at age 18 to when he killed himself at 23, he never sought or received any psychological counseling during his years of service. His story is typical. Most service members receive no psychological treatment or intervention during their service, whether before, during, or after.

Pre-Screening and Suicide Prevention

Nock et al. (2008), in their article on suicide among soldiers, emphasize that suicide rates among soldiers have increased measurably over the past several years and are now the 16th leading cause of death worldwide and the 10th in the United States population. Only recently (beginning in 2008) has this rate of increase exceeded that of civilians.

Hopelessness and sleep disturbance are among the stressors for suicide. Up to 25 percent of U.S. military personnel who returned from deployment to OIF (Operation *Iraqi Freedom*) and OEF (Operation *Enduring Freedom*) reported psychological problems, which can raise the probability of suicide risk among those service members (Hoge et al., 2006). A dreadful reminder of such risk, in 2009 within the first month after the 101st Airborne returned from Afghanistan, there were 10 suicides.

Young soldiers who return from the theater of combat can be subject to severe deterioration of their emotional stability when they hear one of their closest comrades has fallen. This was the case for HR, a 24-year-old infantry soldier I attended to at a U.S. field hospital in Europe following his medivac from Iraq. His eyes revealed a stare into emptiness, a face filled with hopelessness. His utterances were barely audible but unquestionably words of despair. His identity was hanging by a thread, and thoughts of a purposeless life consumed his soul. The last straw: his best battle buddy had just put an M-16 to his chest and pulled the trigger. He wanted to do the same and end the misery of his disconnected self. This was his burden too heavy to bear; he was a hollow shell of a young man with a thousand-yard stare.

While deployed in 2008, during OEF, in one of my several European assignments, I was assigned to the only U.S. military field hospital left in Europe, an enormous medical facility serving 22 military contingencies. It was not uncommon to see numerous ambulance buses arrive daily full of casualties. In my journal I recorded, "'They're inbound, and their plane has touched down, three coming from Iraq,' barks the Navy lieutenant, this is my second weekend in a row to be on call." There were actually four from Iraq and Afghanistan. The Navy lieutenant sent two to the hospital:

> The undiagnosed young airman will probably not survive his military career. Still, he will be a healthier man and husband to his newlywed wife and unborn son as he complies to continue on mood stabilizers. One soldier from Balad, Iraq, was a sad case with a long history of ADHD and anger management issues since age 6. Being dumped by his fiancée was the last straw. Before my call was over, I was up till nearly midnight working on the three patients who were left over from other referrals. A walk through the three miles of hallways bore witness to young, innocent faces, some with no legs or arms, or loss of eyesight. I solemnly bowed my head, wishing that I could make it go away.

Personality traits such as impulsiveness, aggressiveness, and hopelessness are ominous challenges in the face of performance expectations in the military. Wood, in her review of military suicides (July 17, 2002), states that young men ages 17–25 in the military were twice as likely to commit suicide as their civilian peers, based on the analysis of death certificates. Some cannot take the pressure even of boot camp. When a sergeant tells you, "Push, push, push through your pain," this mantra can translate as, "Don't look weak, suck it up," which builds resistance to any admission of mental health problems. This might bring shame and self-denigration.

Consequently, many of these young soldiers have refused to see mental health professionals even in times of crisis. Too often, the military mantra had been, "You are either completely broken, or you just suck it up."

In 2012, speaking to fellow House members, Representative Jim McDermott identified military suicides as an "epidemic." He asserted that what progress is being made in suicide prevention would only be "fleeting" if the Army and the country at large did not reduce the "stigma" which accompanies active-duty service members when they seek behavioral health treatment.

A poignant example is illustrated when a recruit enters the military and is psychologically ill-prepared, and no one is listening. For one private, the basic training "suck-it-up" mantra ignored a reality check. On admission to a field hospital, his statement was very telling:

> I was trying to tell people in basic that I was having problems. Then I didn't get to see anyone until AT [Advanced Training]. I was depressed when I signed up. I listen to a lot of people here and all the problems they have when they come back from Iraq. And I have them problems too, but I haven't even been there yet. That means that I probably will have to double the problems. Sometimes I wished that someone would end it for me. Like if I went to Iraq, I wouldn't even care if I got shot. The other problem is that I could get someone killed by not caring.

Many 17- and 18-year-olds fighting in Vietnam had enlisted with conviction and passion for answering the call of America's most divisive war. As time passed, many experienced uncertainties about why they were there. This measurably impacted their vulnerable morale. It is important to remember that the Army medical policy for draftees deployed to Vietnam was fundamentally, "Anyone can take anything for a year." This especially did not bode well for the draftees, most of whom were ambivalent or noncommittal towards the war effort. Thus, they were not received by the enlistees with the same comradeliness, morale became an even more serious problem for them.

The antithesis for Corporal Musgrave with the 3rd Marine Division, is aptly portrayed in my interview with him in 2022:

> [The division] took, the most casualties of any unit in the history of the Marine Corps... The Walking Dead... When I was 17, the ink wasn't even dry on my

diploma... I've been waiting to go in since I was a little kid... But after I came home and saw what a clusterfuck it turned to... You feel lucky you were there when you still had the illusion of victory... You felt more welcomed home when you returned to Vietnam a few weeks ago than you ever felt when you came from the war in the late 60s.

Even those who were career soldiers became greatly conflicted, as described by Patience H. C. Mason in her book *Recovering from the War* (1990):

For many career men, the conduct of the war in Vietnam, the body counts, the lack of unit cohesiveness, the inability to win due to the rules of that particular war and the political situation (most of the Vietnamese who were willing to lay down their lives seemed to be on the other side), combined sometime with the desire for military glory and sometimes with simple patriotism, made it impossible for them. They ceased to think. It was too painful. They ceased to feel; that was also too painful.

Author H. J. Glover, in his article in the *Journal of Mental Disorders* (1988), speaks to the events during combat when a battle buddy dies. Such an event can render the surviving comrades vulnerable to survivor's guilt and depression. And when combat soldiers come from a problematic childhood, they can reexperience old feelings of guilt and succumb to intractable depression and suicidality.

In some cases, the service member can be rehabilitated by being placed on a "profile" (a temporary restriction from deployment) for a specified time while in treatment. This approach can help to treat psychological wounds, by, for example, ensuring no active-duty assignments in theaters where the patient might be triggered and where inpatient facilities are unavailable.

Overcoming psychological trauma is a process that involves developing a will to be proactive along with an ability to regulate emotions and stay anchored in the present. Building positive relationships and mentoring has also served as an adjunct to success for military veterans who have overcome their past demons.

Those with unrelenting chronic post-trauma symptoms may experience lingering torment for years. This is illustrated in another interview with a veteran, the son of a third-generation military father: "I used to say,

'Dad, you cannot drink so much.' He said, 'Son, I see every person I ever killed before I go to sleep, and I have to sort of have a part of a drink for every one of them.'" Fathers suffering with PTSD can also be troublesome for their children. They may become fearful, anxious and depressed. A recent CBS 60 Minutes newscast, "Children of Veterans with PTSD," aired on April 28, 2024, and narrated by Aaron Weiz, highlights the heartbreaking reality of children who have become caregivers for their fathers returning home with PTSD from having served in Iraq and Afghanistan. Many of the children, having to bear a great responsibility at such a young age, are not only faced with the challenges of caring for their fathers but also with their own struggles of fear, anxiety and depression, some becoming suicidal. It begs the question, could PTSD become contagious?

Author John Musgrave, in his memoir of surviving Vietnam (2021), shares his struggle:

> The biggest thing I had to deal with after my time in the Marine Corps, I often told Soldiers, was survivor's guilt, though I didn't learn the name for it until years later. Every day I struggled with the question of why I was still alive and my buddies weren't. I was ashamed of surviving.

An interview with one battled-tested Vietnam veteran illuminates residual, still to this day, demons from his past:

> They teach you to be a killing machine... take a kid's life, a woman's life, a dog's life. And so, you go in there, and you go in, and you wipe out a whole village, and then you have to live with that. And so, they expect you to come back into society and be a normal person. You're not a normal person... So, I just think that there's, there's just still a lot of our veterans that are really screwed up... PTSD, and so, I just told her (his wife), I said, you know, there's gonna be times that I'm gonna be, just want to be by myself.

Further attestation to the long and unforgiving effects of combat trauma, after 50-plus years, is seen through the lens of 82-year-old Vietnam veteran Colonel Marty Strones, a Silver Star awardee:

> When you look at the first person in combat, in the eyes of that person, and kill them, that changes you forever. And you never end that, especially when the killing continues. I never really talked about the war to anybody. But inside, I had to carry all that stuff with me.

Stress and PTSD

Twenty years after the end of the Vietnam War, 15.2 percent of U.S. Vietnam veterans continued to suffer from PTSD. It can be a long and difficult road back to health for many. Unfortunately, chronicity has its sinister way of keeping track and staying stuck.

A study published in *Psychological Science* underscores soldiers who enlisted before age 25 and served in combat, to be seven times more likely to develop PTSD syndrome than those who were 25 and older (Dohrenwend et al., 2013). Severity of combat exposure was the strongest predictor of the syndrome. Adding two factors—pre-war vulnerability and harming the innocent—veterans have a 97 percent chance of developing PTSD following combat.

Maguen and Norman, in their paper on moral injury (published in *PTSD Research Quarterly*, 2022), investigate the moral injury suffered by veterans who have killed and who carry a stigma. They cite programs that confront the impact of killing, and which emphasize self-forgiveness and spiritual strength building.

The Army, in its attempt to prepare troops for battle, set forth its "Comprehensive Soldier Fitness" (CSF) program noted in the *New York Times* article (March 2012). The CSF is a tailored virtual and classroom training program by resilience experts to teach critical skills to soldiers as well as their families. This policy has received much criticism for suggesting that a soldier's commitment to a higher purpose is the mission first, which makes for resiliency. No reputable psychologist or psychiatrist would deny that the majority of people who are capable of such a commitment also possess empathy for others and, thus, implicit moral values. Those who suffer moral injury are at increased risk for suicide.

Much has been portrayed through the autobiography and films of the British Army World War II veteran Eric Lomax, who suffered severe psychological trauma and torment after extensive and repetitive torture by his captor in a Japanese POW camp. His suffering did not end until 30 years after he returned to the camp and discovered forgiveness in confronting his captor.

Many people view stress and PTSD as interchangeable terms. However, stress is not always a precursor to PTSD. Some experience severe stress and never develop PTSD. For any mental health disorder cause is complex, especially the exact relationships between stress, traumatic experiences, and subsequent psychiatric disorders.

Neurobiological scientists explain this based on a neurotransmitter—a chemical messenger that crosses the synaptic gap between neurons and helps relay information between the brain and body. We know some of the neurotransmitters involved in PTSD include serotonin, norepinephrine, and dopamine. And many remain to be discovered. Neuroscience research has found that blocking the stress-response circuitry with a beta blocker like Inderal can inhibit the neurotransmitter noradrenaline. Noradrenaline normally stimulates the hypothalamus and prefrontal cortex, which in turn activate the combat-tuned amygdala. The amygdala is the part of the brain that can cause combat veterans to have an exaggerated startle response to stimuli such as car backfires or firecrackers. With the beta blocker inhibiting this pathway, the veteran is less likely to have an extreme reaction, such as diving to the ground when hearing a loud noise. This inhibition helps prevent embarrassment and overreactions. More research is still needed, but using beta blockers prophylactically shows promise for reducing PTSD induced by combat situations.

Men and women who have experienced traumatic stress during military service have an increased risk for psychiatric symptoms. These symptoms may include PTSD, depression, anxiety, and substance abuse.

When resistance to and escape from terror are not possible, consciousness tends to be fragmented and disorganized, as if the mind, to handle the spectacle of one's annihilation, has to slice up consciousness into smaller, more manageable pieces (Morris, 2015). These broken parts lead to dissociation, which serves as a protective mechanism during intense or overwhelming fear, but the implications down the road are crippling. When dissociation occurs in the absence of trauma, one can behave as if they have a split identity and react to ordinary situations as if they represent the terror of their traumatic event.

For example, a Vietnam war veteran may hear a helicopter overhead and duck, or an Afghanistan war veteran drives down the highway and believes the trucks passing him are tanks, reliving the moment of being in combat. Morris believes these major traumas are both a death and a rebirth—that is, an end of one kind of consciousness and the beginning of another.

Army psychiatrist Dr. Hoge, who studied PTSD and the effects of treatment, states, "The bottom line is that there is no 'magic bullet' for PTSD, and claims to the contrary should not be taken with more than a grain of salt" (2004).

PTSD, by definition, is one of several anxiety disorders. Most clinicians would agree with J. Herman, author of "Trauma and Recovery" (1997), that the majority of symptoms fall into a triad: "hyperarousal, intrusion, constriction." In my clinical work with PTSD, I have observed the traumatized individual startles easily and reacts with irritability to minor provocation and struggles with avoidance, isolation, insomnia, self-loathing, stuck in a "cerebral foxhole," not to mention other symptomatology. It has left emotional scars on many soldiers who have borne the battle, resulting in physical and emotional wounds. Recovery from PTSD can be as high as 80 percent if treatment is completed. However, this is not a guarantee. Early recognition and treatment of symptoms are critical to the prevention of chronicity.

PTSD can be a major factor contributing to suicide and has no boundaries for its victims. Yet, it's the unwelcome gift that keeps on giving. A recent painful and tragic reminder is the death of Navy SEAL Mike Day, an Iraq scout survivor. Through his heroic efforts, he took down four terrorist leaders but not before being shot 27 times. He took his life on March 28, 2023, leaving behind a legacy to be read in his book, *Perfectly Wounded*. After the Iraq war, he lived his years giving to others, with care programs to help other service members. With all the work Mike put in to treat his crippling depression and give back to others, PTSD ultimately won the battle.

A recent cohort study of 57,841 active-duty service members with combat duty in Iraq/Afghanistan, reveals the majority of those who attempted suicide had been diagnosed with PTSD (LeardMann et al., 2021).

In my years as a psychiatrist, I have met veterans who served in Vietnam, many of whom still refuse to share their histories of war trauma. Instead, the painful memories lie dormant in their soul, wounds that have been only partially closed, like a festering sore that never goes away.

Vietnam-era Army surgeon Crile Doscher in a 2022 interview, echoes the sentiment:

> I have pretty biased opinions about PTSD because I experienced it myself, and it's never gone away. And I can't imagine how a young person at 19 years old, let's say the average age for a combat soldier, who sees death and people mangled by explosives, copes with it. I think it's a forever thing. As they grow older, I think these young people have vivid memories of those who have lost limbs and just mind-boggling injuries. I don't think that ever disappears.

Burdens of Stress for the Medical Corps

> Pain is attracted by these things. She is a harlot in the pay of War, and she amuses herself with the wreckage of men. She consorts with decay, addicted to blood, cohabits with mutilations, and her delight is the refuse of suffering bodies. (Borden, 1929)

> She listened to his cries all night, for the morphia brought him no relief. Morphia gives a little relief, at times, from the pain of life, but it is only death that brings absolute relief. (La Motte, 2019)

World War II Army Nurse June Wandrey, author of *Bedpan Commando* (1989), tells of the tragic carnage she witnessed in the taking of Monte Cassino in 1944: "It was a beautiful, sobering sight, I still see the faces of all those healthy, vital young men who were maimed and killed trying to take the area."

Can treating battle wounds in a hospital setting trigger PTSD? Civilians might assume that doctors, nurses, and other medical personnel are toughened by years of training to handle the most gruesome and brutal cases. But sadly, that's not true. For as long as wars have been fought, medical personnel have been as vulnerable to PTSD and other psychological disorders as the soldiers they treat.

It is not only soldiers who fight in battles who are scarred for life. The French nurses who cared for the wounded at the front in World War I were challenged with the horrific stress of war and futile attempts to save young soldiers whose lives were hanging by a thread. In an attempt to rationalize or justify the hopelessness of these dying young men's sacrifice, some caregivers burned out and, at wit's end, were tempted with jaded thoughts, as illustrated in Higonnet's book *Nurses at the Front* (2001): "I'd rather see a man die in prime of life, in war time, than see him doddering along in peace time, broken hearted, broken spirited, life broken, and very weary, having suffered many things, to die at last, at a good, ripe age!" Having to make such split-second life-and-death decisions carries its own toll.

It is the intervals in war, that space between life and death, that has an unforgiving, cruel, and chilling effect, as aptly explained in *Nurses at the Front*: "He knew he had been decorated in extremis, because he was going to die, and he did not want to die. So, he sobbed and sobbed all the while the General decorated him, and protested that he did not want to die… Death is dignified and life is dignified, but the intervals are awful. They are ludicrous, repulsive."

A casualty hospital at the front in the Iraq War was so full of dead and wounded soldiers it became known as "the Dead Man's Hotel." One of my patients, Chris A., was a 32-year-old burned-out Army nurse having been medivac'd from Iraq. She described her stressful experiences as a combat nurse, tears flowing down her face. "When you see a young, wounded soldier brought in and both arms and legs missing, and after surgical procedures, he is ready for transport. I pick up only a torso, like a baby, and I carry him to the transport for medivac back to the States. I can't take it anymore." Much of her burnout was also related to her stress from witnessing so many children who were victims of collateral damage and those that could not be saved.

Sometimes the intervals, that space between life and death can be a heavy burden to endure for nurses and doctors, too great to overcome. Physicians who try beyond hope to save a service member's life can experience devastation if their efforts fall short, a failure that can be too much to bear. Failure and the Hippocratic oath can present an onerous challenge. For doctors in war zones, the pressure to respond quickly to emergencies while maintaining their mental and emotional resources is immense.

A case in point goes back to the Vietnam War. I conferred with an ex-Army psychiatrist in Bangkok, who had been discharged. He tried to keep his war trauma to himself. He had been drafted out of residence training and sent straight to Vietnam, unaware that he would be placed at the front as a surgeon to face the surgical challenges of combat wounds.

I visited him at his home in California approximately 30 years after the war. Although it was decades later, the war stayed with him, seared into his psyche, doubtful that he ever recovered from his PTSD.

There are many causes of burnout among military doctors. Primary reasons include extensive/multiple deployments, rigorous and fast-paced work, long and irregular hours, no time off, and a lack of support from superiors or coworkers. Additionally, military doctors often experience high stress levels and repeated exposure to traumatic events.

The significant stress for Army surgical nurses caring for the wounded likely comes from the uncertainty of their patients' recoveries. The extent of the service member's injury, the complexity of the surgical procedure, and the continuous influx of injured service men and women require constant vigilance.

For military surgeons, combat wounds can be complicated for many reasons. They can be caused by bullets, shrapnel, IEDs, or other projectiles. They can infect tissue and blood, and they can require extensive surgery. Some more complex combat wounds include traumatic brain injuries, spinal cord injuries, and amputations. Organ and vascular wounds can be particularly challenging and may require the assistance of specialized surgeons, which are few in number. In addition, knowing that a patient could be saved but for one's lack of skill or training often causes medical personnel to carry with them guilt and shame that never goes away. Because they are medical "professionals," they believe that they should never have such feelings. They may have never even set foot on a battlefield, so how can they have PTSD? As a psychiatrist who has met scores of doctors and nurses who were traumatized by treating critically injured soldiers, I can definitively state that no one is immune, no matter how tough, intelligent, resilient, or well trained.

In E. N. La Motte's book, *The Backwash of War* (2019), she depicts the raw and graphic carnage of World War I combat wounds, of tragic cases that the surgeons, along with her and other nurses, witnessed daily in a field hospital in France:

> Across the lad's forehead was a black silk bandage, which could be removed later, and in his pocket, there was an address from which artificial eyes might be purchased... Antoine looked down upon this wreck of his son that lay before

him, and the wreck, not appreciating that he was a surgical triumph, kept sobbing, kept weeping out of his sightless eyes, kept jerking his four stumps in supplication, kept begging in agony: "Kill me, Papa!"

Burdens Too Heavy to Bear for Civilian Military (DOD) Employees

It's easy not to think about civilian employees working for the military. They are overlooked because they are neither members of the Armed Services nor are they accorded the rights and privileges of being in the military. And yet, there are nearly 1 million civilians employed by the Department of Defense (DOD), including more than 300,000 who work on military bases, many of whom serve critical functions that the men and women in uniform can't fulfill. Although they don't carry weapons, they suffer from many of the same issues as the men and women in uniform whom they support.

The most common problems for DOD employees include completing tasks quickly and efficiently, coping with stress and changing conditions (priorities), and maintaining communication with superiors. In addition, some civilians may experience problems interacting with military personnel, particularly their superiors. DOD employees may also be overworked, but this is not an epidemic. Priorities from the upper echelon dictate deadlines. In my experience, these many times exceed the 40-hour-per-week limit, but without being given extra pay, of course, not in line with the Fair Labor Standards Act.

As a consultant on a crucial court martial case and a civilian working for the DOD, I put in 30 hours of extra work for a week beyond my regular 40 hours but received no overtime. Of course, I never complained. There was nowhere to file a grievance. Overtime came with the territory, and I accepted it as such. For physicians, however, there are expectations where they are called upon to work extra hours to provide the needed medical expertise or care in exceptional cases to meet the standard of care.

At the same time, there are numerous examples where DOD staff feel they are taken advantage of by a new replacement supervisor (officer) who prefers to dictate rather than request a particular work assignment or workload and has an unbecoming, bullying manner of supervising. This scenario can set the stage for resentment and distrust, leading to a hostile relationship between the person wearing the uniform and the civilian employee who is outside of the "fraternity." If this is not checked and corrected, it can lead to staff burnout and end up at the behest of Human Resources or the legal system.

A pharmacist I had worked with over the years was knowledgeable, confident, and capable in her expertise and was eventually promoted to a supervisor position. However, a year after a newly assigned LTC replaced her superior, I witnessed an emotional deterioration in her demeanor, with depressive symptoms. Around the same time, a vacancy occurred in the pharmacy staff, which was left unfilled. Her new boss (more likely than not unsuited for the position) mandated that she be responsible for two jobs (full-time supervisor and unfilled staff position). She was leaving work by 9:00 every night, not sleeping well, had constant fatigue, and was never receiving any thanks or appreciation for her extra duty hours. The new replacement was also undermining the general morale of other staff. She could no longer tolerate the toxic environment and, after obtaining legal counsel, filed a lawsuit against the Department of Defense. She won her case, and the DOD paid her legal fees with strict stipulations for her workload and chain-of-command limits. Cases like hers are, fortunately, rare. During most of my years with the DOD, I had with few exceptions, superiors who were respectful, supportive, and genuinely appreciative of civilian staff's contribution to the mission and service to the military.

Another area of conflict surfaces when military protocol/ethics clash with those of DOD employees with regard to the management and care of inpatients. This can be a major juggernaut when it involves the DOD physician's ethical standards, which conflict with the military's highest echelon priorities. On a more personal level, this brings to light my most stressful encounter with military bureaucracy.

During Operation *Desert Storm* (Gulf War), I volunteered as a civilian physician to go overseas and help support the casualty hospital in Nuremberg, Germany (98th General Army Hospital). Within six months of my arrival in Germany, I was promoted to chief of inpatient psychiatry service. One of the casualties from the Gulf War was an officer,

NB, who was in the neuro-med ward, diagnosed with organic brain syndrome and delirium, and then transferred to the inpatient psychiatry ward. The CID attempted to interrogate an incompetent patient with a debilitating brain syndrome with delirium, dementia, psychosis, and severe depression. What happened next could fill an entire book on the conflict between medical ethics and military expediency.

While different from those in uniform, the burdens placed on civilian DOD employees are still quite real. As a civilian physician working overseas on an Army base during the Gulf War, I witnessed the immense pressure cooker these assignments can become. The stakes are high. Lives hang in the balance, and the chain of command rules supreme. Mistakes or misjudgments can haunt you forever, as I learned firsthand.

Yet those burdens must be borne for the sake of the greater mission. As a civilian, I did not take an oath to support and defend the Constitution as military members do. However, by accepting that assignment during a time of war, I still had an obligation to care for the service members under my charge to the best of my abilities. That required adhering to my ethical principles even when it put me at odds with my military superiors.

The case of NB I mentioned earlier perfectly encapsulates the potential clashes between military expediency and civilian notions of professional ethics. However, there are countless similar examples that civilian DOD personnel face every day, albeit with lower stakes. We are tasked with finding ways to fulfill the mission while still upholding our own moral codes. That is not always an easy balancing act.

Nowadays, with the U.S. no longer engaged in major combat operations, those types of dilemmas arise less frequently. But the potential remains whenever civilian DOD staff are embedded closely with warfighters in conflict zones. It is imperative that proper training and oversight exist to help mitigate any ethical lapses. The Pentagon seems to recognize this, as evidenced by the recent emphasis on programs to include teaching ethics.

Of course, training alone is insufficient. We must also foster a climate where speaking truth to power is valued, not penalized. My experience showed me that the chain of command does not always appreciate constructive pushback from below. Yet that feedback is essential to avoid groupthink and poor decision-making. The healthiest organizations empower dissenting voices.

In the civilian world, we take for granted certain whistleblower protections and the ability to resign from jobs without retribution. Those options are far more constrained within the military hierarchy that civilian DOD personnel must navigate. It requires treading carefully, picking battles wisely, and, above all, maintaining perspective. The mission always comes first, even when we disagree with some aspects of its execution.

Overall, I emerged from my time as a civilian DOD employee with a much greater appreciation for the sacrifices and pressures inherent in military service. Though my burden was heavy at times, it pales next to what many in uniform shoulder daily. In our comfort and safety, we owe them all a tremendous debt. I only hope that those burdens can be lightened wherever possible for service members and civilians alike. The mission deserves no less.

More Stresses Faced by Active-duty Service Members and Veterans

Military sexual trauma (MST) has become an epidemic that exacts a severe psychological toll on victims. Studies estimate around 1 in 4 women and 1 in 100 men are sexually assaulted during their military service (Protect Our Defenders, 2018). These estimations are further quantified by a 2022 research publication that highlights the prevalence of MST among male and female veterans at 3.5 percent and 44.2 percent (Nichter et al., 2022). This trauma is directly linked to conditions like PTSD, depression, substance abuse, and suicide (Katz, 2016). Women veterans are nearly nine times more likely to develop PTSD from MST than combat exposure (Dutra et al., 2010). Yet due, to stigma, underreporting is rampant. We must confront MST openly, provide better support systems, and prosecute perpetrators to protect those who swear to defend America.

Likewise, bullying and hazing—though officially prohibited—remain stubborn fixtures in military culture that can breed mental health issues. Young, enlisted members and perceived outsiders are frequent targets.

Minorities, in particular, may have to deal with added stress from discrimination and racial slurs. A 2014 Pentagon survey revealed 55 percent of minority service members suffered racial harassment, impacting their job performance and morale (Gould, 2014). The fear of appearing weak dissuades reporting. While recent diversity initiatives, such as inclusive recruitment and hiring practices, are a step forward, leaders must set the tone from the top that bigotry will not be tolerated. No one should feel sidelined for their identity while serving the nation that espouses equal opportunity.

Unfortunately, the problems people face inside the military can be just as bad or worse once they leave service. The systems meant to support veterans are themselves buckling under the strain. A tidal wave of PTSD disability claims has overwhelmed the Veterans Affairs Department. Their backlog reached over 600,000 in 2013, with veterans waiting over 250 days on average for decisions. Appeals can add years more to that purgatory. Meanwhile, VA facilities often lack the capacity to meet demand. Exhausted veterans pursuing treatment face understaffing, long waits for appointments, and substandard care.

Approximately 11–20 percent of Iraq and Afghanistan veterans have PTSD, but less than half seek treatment (Friedman, 2015). Barriers include stigma, lack of understanding, and frustration navigating bureaucratic obstacles. Abandoned and unable to cope, many turn to substance abuse. Veterans are twice as likely to die from accidental overdoses than civilians (Tsai, 2013) Tragically, 20 veterans take their own lives every day, a suicide rate 1.5 times higher than the general population (Kemp and Bossarte, 2012). Among post-9/11 veterans, the numbers are even more troubling, with young male vets twice as likely to die from suicide compared to their civilian peers (Kang et al., 2015).

Homelessness is another tragic outcome where systems are failing. Although veterans make up only 7 percent of the U.S.'s general population, they account for nearly 13 percent of the homeless (Henry et al., 2017).

Wars take an immense toll, both seen and unseen. PTSD, depression, brain injury, and other challenges can leave veterans displaced and destitute after their service. More must be done to provide housing, health care, job training, and other support. We cannot simply wave the flag when troops deploy and discard them afterward. True patriotism means caring for veterans at their lowest—in memory of their willingness to sacrifice everything for us.

Burdens Too Heavy to Bear for Families

My career as a psychologist began amid the Vietnam War, providing diagnostic treatment for military families stationed in Bangkok. Despite its reputation as a haven, the city posed profound challenges for residents.

One such challenge was the rampant opiate abuse among teenage boys, most struggling with their fathers' prolonged absence on the war's frontlines. Preoccupied with wartime duties and advancing their military careers, too many of these fathers had left their sons back home rudderless, in a void devoid of parental guidance or discipline. Their wives, known colloquially as "nine-month widows," were left to bear the brunt of this absence alone, constantly struggling to balance their children's needs against the backdrop of a nation bitterly divided over the controversial ethics of the ongoing war.

Take the cautionary tale of 16-year-old Kenny. His father, an ambitious lieutenant colonel, was laser-focused on getting promoted to the esteemed "eagle" rank of full colonel. When Kenny realized his father prioritized climbing the military ladder over providing for his basic well-being and emotional needs, the seeds of adolescent rebellion took root. The boy subsequently began experimenting with marijuana as an act of defiance, along with other wayward teens. But what started as relatively harmless, dabbling in cannabis, soon devolved into regular heroin abuse and full-blown addiction.

At the time, heroin was cheap at just $5 per hit and easily accessible from local noodle vendors and taxi drivers. It quickly became the drug of choice for neglected and unsupervised teens like Kenny, who, craving attention and escape, turned to the warm embrace of opiates to fill the painful parental void in their lives. Yet Kenny's mother remained stubbornly in denial about his burgeoning substance abuse problem and his downward spiral into addiction, despite increasingly clear and unmistakable signs of his impairment—showing up to school high as a kite, slurring his words, wearing a vacant, disconnected gaze. She consistently overlooked all the obvious red flags signaling her son's self-destructive trajectory, either consciously denying reality to preserve her peace of mind or subconsciously rationalizing away the facts rather than directly confronting the painful truth head-on. However, any confirmed drug abuse or addiction issues arising within a military family foreshadowed a devastating career blow for the service member's father—typically resulting in the entire family being shipped back stateside prematurely under administrative disciplinary action. Yet even after the school counselor urgently referred Kenny to an Army substance abuse counselor for formal evaluation, his mother stubbornly failed to show up for the counseling appointment.

Tragically, Kenny's story ended abruptly one fateful morning when his distraught mother found her son lifeless in his bedroom—yet another tragic casualty of the insidious scourge of opiate addiction. The medical examiner concluded Kenny had fatally overdosed by combining a highly potent batch of heroin with a powerful sedative. This lethal combination shuts down the brain's respiratory control center, almost invariably causing sudden death by asphyxiation. Kenny was just one of many similar teen casualties at his high school that year alone. Within 18 months, a staggering 12 students from Kenny's graduating class had died prematurely, preventable deaths after mixing this same deadly drug cocktail.

What is the common thread linking these heartbreaking tragedies? Upon closer examination, investigators found many of these troubled teens came from military families lacking close interpersonal bonds and mutual understanding. Often, their parents found themselves inadequately prepared to navigate the profound culture shock and unique challenges associated with raising teenagers in a foreign country brimming with enticing vices. They displayed a paradoxical style of parenting that was overly protective at home while surprisingly permissive when their children socialized in local hangouts, even including, on rare occasions, bars or nightclubs frequented by GIs. Unintentionally, these family dynamics resulted in a precarious absence of necessary parental structure, attention, engagement, and guidance at home. Moreover, some parents' rigid adherence to the prevailing prejudices against Thailand meant that their children were denied experiencing the richness of Thai culture, such as its cuisine, language, mores, and events, which might have helped mitigate their rebellious behavior.

It is well established through extensive research that a successful military career requires exceptional devotion, personal sacrifice, physical courage, and moral character. Yet a service member's ultimate success or failure often hinges largely on the level of emotional support and daily practical assistance freely provided by their relatives back home. Both standout accomplishments and lackluster washout rates in military service can usually be traced directly back to the degree of positive involvement, empathetic understanding of military life demands, and active encouragement supplied by service members' families.

For example, in his seminal 1984 research paper, military psychologist Dr. Robert Schneider, MA, PhD, LTC (Ret.), Vietnam-era veteran stationed in Bangkok, Chief, Department of Neuropsychiatry, vividly emphasized the manifold harmful consequences of sustained family discord on combat readiness and battlefield performance:

> For the vast majority of enlisted soldiers and officers alike, ongoing serious worries about problems or deficiencies back on the home front can be a major source of severe psychological distress. These persistent concerns inevitably jeopardize the individual soldier's ability to adequately participate in, absorb, retain, and implement the critical training activities designed to prepare them for combat operations. Most critically, from a national defense perspective, preoccupations with turbulent home front matters severely interfere with soldiers' ability to perform their complex combat-related duties effectively and safely on the battlefield. Such constant worries and distractions place the preoccupied soldier and their fellow unit members at significantly higher risk of casualty and death. In addition, these pervasive distractions about difficulties back home severely threaten the likelihood of successful mission completion and markedly increase the risk that the stressed soldier will suffer psychological breakdown when confronted by the extreme duress of combat.

In stark contrast, among service members able to sustain long, successful military careers, their families back home have generally provided vital stability by acting as emotional anchors. Military spouses and parents can offer essential motivation during adversity and engender a profound sense of love, purpose, and belonging within the military community. Families of successful personnel also handle critical practical matters on the home front with competence and grace—such as managing household finances, raising children, and maintaining the family residence. They are dutiful and deliberate in maintaining strong communication channels to nurture family rapport and prevent emotional distance, even when the service member is deployed overseas or sent on remote assignments for months.

Conversely, those service members who suffered abbreviated, unsuccessful military careers often point to a lack of adequate family support as the primary reason, if not the sole underlying cause, for their poor performance and premature washout from service. Without a basic appreciation for the scope of unique challenges and demands inherent to the military family lifestyle, their relatives back home often failed to provide the requisite level of emotional empathy, understanding, and day-to-day practical support. As a result, rather than uplifting the service member, families frequently unintentionally isolate them, causing the service member to feel helplessly alone and abandoned. This destructive emotional and physical separation can often lead to sharply declining morale, a lackluster effort by service members in training and service duties, and deep disillusionment and dissatisfaction with military life. Additionally, routine family-related stressors encountered back home—such as financial pressures, marital tensions, parenting disputes, and adolescent behavioral issues—can further preoccupy and demoralize a service member from afar, severely hampering their ability to serve effectively under challenging circumstances.

Although the Department of Defense may have found a reasonable military justification for its policy of reassigning or "rotating" service members to new duty stations every few years, the cost to the stability and mental health of the affected families is often overlooked or disregarded. According to former Army psychiatrist Richard Schneider, Col. (Ret.), this repetitive uprooting and juggling of the lives of military dependents is one of the most frequent reasons for mental health service requests:

> Such requests usually result from fracturing friendships and relationships, spousal employment being disrupted, academic pursuits and pathways being derailed, and community involvements and commitments being terminated. During our attempts to help families sort out these dilemmas and minimize the cost to their mental health that these repetitive "rotation orders" present, it is hard not to recall one of the Army's oft-told apocryphal stories. A soldier described to his commanding officer the impact that another move was about to have on his wife and adolescent children and was told, "Sergeant, if the Army wanted you to have a family to worry about, they would have issued you one."

The Impact of Deployment on the Family

In addition to the continuous strain of family separation, deployments away from the home front present yet another significant emotional challenge for military families already weighed down by the sacrifices of military life. Anxiety, stress, uncertainty, and dread permeate the household before, during, and after prolonged overseas deployments. The looming specter of a dangerous deployment generates intense emotional anguish. It frequently manifests in ancillary mental health issues, including depression, sleep disturbances, increased aggression, marital conflict, and other psychological well-being disruptions in service members and their stateside families. Military spouses and children left at home bear the particularly heavy brunt of a deployed service member's absence. These family members struggle to construct a new post-deployment "normal" within their fractured, reconstituted social-family dynamic. Forced to take on unfamiliar roles and responsibilities, they often feel isolated and abandoned when the service member deploys.

Likewise, despite strong anticipation, a service member's return home after finally completing an overseas combat deployment is rarely the joyous occasion one might expect after such a protracted absence under extremely arduous conditions. Military families often report feeling conflicted as months or years apart inevitably change perspectives and priorities on both sides. The numerous emotional and relationship changes that naturally evolved on the home front during a deployment frequently lead to feelings of alienation, anger, bitterness, and loss of autonomy and control in the returning service member. This situation requires an extended period of challenging emotional adjustment for the service member and their stateside family members. Each side struggles to accept the "new normal" until intimacy and stability can gradually be re-established.

Moreover, the relentless accumulation of repeated overseas deployments over multiple years represents an incredibly taxing experience that can push military couples to the breaking point, even relationships that once seemed solid and resilient. The sustained cycle of recurring extended deployments introduces a pervasive element of uncertainty, chronic stress, and emotional disruption that can profoundly strain intimate bonds between spouses as well as parent–child bonds. In environments where constant deployment has become normalized, persistent moods of bitterness, anger, resentment, and mistrust on both sides often slowly supplant the warmth, empathy, passion, and mutual understanding that previously characterized the relationship during periods of stability. Indeed, even in the healthiest marriages, corrosive emotions, including anger, jealousy, and sexual infidelity, may gradually take root and fester in this high-stress, long-distance environment, wherein one partner continuously shoulders all household and childrearing burdens alone at home. At the same time, their spouse spends months or years absorbed in their intense duty overseas. The dependent spouse often feels overwhelmed and alone, while the deployed service member feels increasingly isolated from their family. Young married couples are especially vulnerable to stress in their relationship as the initial deployment begins. Loneliness comes first, followed by resentment. Then anger erodes trust—infidelity may even slip in and encroach on some of the most solid marriages. In some cases, the caustic influence of separation moves the needle further to temptation. Yet, we are all considered free moral agents, and there is accountability for decisions.

This destructive emotional dynamic has become commonplace and pernicious in recent decades, as more young married military personnel with families have been compelled to cycle through multiple grueling combat tours and prolonged overseas deployments, especially throughout the wars in Iraq and Afghanistan. Compared to the draft forces utilized in earlier wars like Vietnam and Korea, the modern all-volunteer force skews much younger demographically. As a result, dramatically higher percentages of currently deployed service members in the Iraq and Afghan wars left wives, infant children, and young families at home alone while deployed—nearly twice the proportion compared to the Vietnam era. Psychiatrist Dr. Charles Hoge, former director of the Division of Psychiatry and Neuroscience at Walter Reed Army Institute of Research, noted in his testimony in 2006 before the House Veterans Affairs Subcommittee, "Longer deployments, multiple deployments, greater time away from base camps, and combat intensity all contribute to higher rates of PTSD, depression, and marital problems. Yet, during Vietnam, only 20 percent of the soldiers constituted the core of young marriages."

Serving husbands and wives returning home after 12 to 15 months of deployment are usually exuberant about reuniting with their spouse, but for some, it can be other than a second honeymoon. Rather than a storybook reunion of joy, reconnection, and passion, the returning combat veteran often requires an extended period of quiet decompression to begin processing and integrating their traumatic experiences in the war zone. Meanwhile, military spouses on the home front have often reached breaking point while parenting solo, contending with months or years of resentment, loneliness, and mistrust after holding down the fort alone. Particularly young spouses often have not anticipated that the post-deployed spouse is not ready for "business as usual," especially the time needed to decompress from the ravages of theater. Moreover, adaptation to the civilian world requires a paradigm shift from the battlefield to the home front. Thus, returning service members are usually not in sync to fully embrace their usual roles in the family constellation. Achieving full emotional reconnection and marital intimacy requires abundant open communication, tremendous patience, and an unshakable long-term commitment—wellsprings that can run dry for couples stretched to the brink by military life sacrifices. Without dogged effort by both partners, intimate relationships fractured by repeated deployment often continue deteriorating rather than recovering. Feelings of estrangement, frustration, and betrayal accumulate, planting seeds of lasting destruction.

Whether newlyweds or long-term partners, the consequences of such daunting challenges have often not been fully anticipated, and the couple has not had proper preparation for coping. Moreover, our most prolonged wars in the 21st century, with two-to-three 12-month successive deployments, are unlike those of the 20th century, where fewer deployments (usually only one) were the norm.

From my deployment overseas, I recall seeing an anxious and depressed young wife of an airborne soldier in Europe in 2008. They had been married for five years but shared the same roof for only six months. On balance, their marriage was consumed by three long deployments. However, after the second deployment, the homecoming was different. Both spouses realized that the short home interim was just another preparation for the next deployment.

A significant change or a culmination of more minor changes in the spouses' perceptions may become the tipping point for a marital crisis. Still, for many, it's the third deployment that can become the breaking point. This situation leads to emotional exhaustion. The wife may become distant and cold or no longer interested in the husband and instead be preoccupied with her job, which brings about a new role and more independence. The new situation may significantly strain the relationship as the husband views her differently and can no longer handle her emotional dissonance.

Research Insights on Deployment Impacts on Spouses and Children

Many detailed empirical research studies have further illuminated the breadth of adverse psychological impacts and worrisome behavior changes exhibited among military children weathering a parent's extended wartime deployment and absence from the home. Across all age groups studied, academic research has revealed widespread sadness, increased anxiety levels, sleep disturbances, appetite changes, and escalating behavioral discipline issues in children separated from a parent deployed overseas for months. Acting-out behaviors include aggression with siblings, disobedience toward the remaining parent, and inappropriate behaviors at school. Additionally, children's coping responses to a parent's deployment tend to follow predictable patterns based on age and developmental stage. The eldest children within military families frequently manifest increased discipline problems coupled with attention-seeking, immature behaviors such as talking back, tantrums, clinging to the remaining parent, or bed-wetting long after outgrowing such phases.

According to renowned psychologist Erik Erikson's influential psycho-social development theory, the parental absence, stress, and disruption of wartime deployment can cause adolescents to spiral into greater emotional volatility, moodiness, risk-taking behaviors, and open rebellion against authority—all resulting from a traumatic short-circuiting of the core adolescent identity-formation process. Such rebellious behavior can have profound long-term consequences on mental health and relationships if not addressed therapeutically.

Major Snodgrass holds his package of MREs while sandwiched between the soon-to-be members of his squad, day one of Officer Basic Course (OBC) training.

Major Snodgrass on the first day of training in the field (Camp Bullis).

Major Snodgrass, with battle buddy (BB) Vickie, in a troop transport to a new location on training day in the field.

Major Snodgrass, in the field, making a call to HQ to inform them of his location.

Members of Alpha Company positioned to listen to instructions while in the field.

An army field tent to accommodate trainees when living in the field.

Armored personnel carrier for the medical corps in the field (Camp Bullis).

Major Snodgrass with BB posing for a photo while standing between their army cots.

Alpha Company trainees lifting a 150 lb manikin over a 6-foot barrier, prior to leaping over it.

Alpha Company trainees demonstrate the barbed-wire crawl while dragging a 150 lb manikin with them.

Major Snodgrass in the field reassembling his 9 mm Beretta army pistol after clearing the two M-16 rifles.

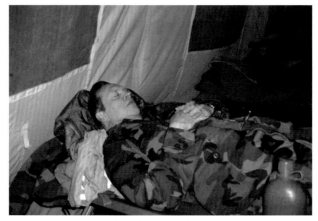

Major Snodgrass lying on his cot in the field tent, exhausted after completing the final obstacle course (litter carry and barbed-wire crawl), moments before being rushed to the emergency room, Brooks Army Medical Center (BAMC).

Major Snodgrass finishing his examination following a series of lectures, Ft. Sam Houston, Texas.

Major Snodgrass poses for a photo while standing in the medical corps equipment room, Ft. Sam Houston.

Major Snodgrass standing with three fellow OBC graduates (two lieutenants, one captain).

Major Snodgrass with members of his unit, following OBC graduation.

Major Snodgrass stands for his formal lieutenant colonel (LTC) pinning by a colonel, commander of the army hospital, Ft. Sill, Oklahoma, 2004.

LTC Snodgrass in his office during work with active-duty soldier patients, Ft. Riley, Kansas, 2005.

LTC Snodgrass in his first assignment overseas, Heidelberg, Germany, 2006.

LTC Snodgrass meets the chief of psychiatry during his active-duty assignment to the U.S. Army hospital in Heidelberg, 2007.

LTC Snodgrass's deployment to Landstuhl, Germany, the largest U.S. Army field hospital in Europe, 2008.

Ambulance buses run day and night to shuttle the med-evac casualties flown in from Iraq/Afghanistan.

LTC Snodgrass waiting for more ambulance buses to arrive from Ramstein Air Base where the med-evac casualties arrive from theater.

Veteran Lanny Snodgrass standing beside John Musgrave, Vietnam veteran, awarded several medals, three Purple Hearts, and author of *The Education of Corporal John Musgrave: Vietnam and its Aftermath*.

Additional studies examining deployment impacts have highlighted issues among children of different ages. Research shows that the youngest cohort of children aged three to 12 exhibit the highest levels of sadness, separation anxiety, fear of abandonment, and the manifestation of distress by the presentation of physical symptoms during a parental absence overseas. Nightmares, enuresis, digestive issues, and sleep disruptions are common. Among the eldest cohort of adolescent children studied, dramatically increased rates of discipline problems at home and school, drug and alcohol experimentation, immature regressive behaviors, and clinical depression were the most frequently reported outcomes during a parent's extended deployment. Minor children of deployed U.S. Army service members overall displayed markedly higher rates of internalizing fear responses such as social isolation and withdrawal, as well as externalizing behaviors such as aggression, rule-breaking, impulsivity, and disruptive conduct at home and school (Kelley et al., 2001). Most alarmingly, these maladaptive coping behaviors often persist and worsen after the deployed parent's safe return home. Without therapeutic intervention, deployment-related trauma can leave lasting scars on military children.

Moreover, as highlighted earlier, Erikson's seminal psychosocial development theory states that the unavoidable parental absence resulting from extended military deployment frequently causes adolescents to spiral into greater emotional volatility, moodiness, poor impulse control, and experimentation with high-risk, authority-defying behaviors— all resulting from a traumatic short-circuiting of the core adolescent identity-formation process. When this predictable reaction is transplanted into a permissive environment rife with unhealthy distractions, as I witnessed firsthand among Bangkok's thriving opiate subculture, the consequences for emotionally vulnerable military teens can be heart-breaking. The cautionary tale of young Kenny represents one of the countless tragic cases brought to my attention.

This extensive body of empirical research powerfully underscores the crucial stabilizing role fulfilled by military service members' families, for better and for worse. The emotional empathy, daily practical support, and unconditional acceptance provided by their relatives and intimate partners back home can significantly influence how service members perceive, engage with, and ultimately withstand the unrelenting demands inherent to a military career. When this vital familial support network either falters or disappears entirely from a service member's life, the detrimental downstream consequences often reverberate for years, both for the individual and the military. Isolated service members experiencing family discord or neglect far too often become discouraged in training, enlistment completion, and lack post-military stability. Conversely, dismissing or overlooking service members' substantial sacrifices—the long separations, the uncertainty of dangerous assignments, and the ever-present specter of death—often breeds profound family discord. This turbulence frequently leaves service members feeling helplessly frustrated, hopelessly isolated, and unable to serve effectively while consumed with worry about their crumbling family lives back home.

The Intergenerational Impact of Military Service on Families

While the primary focus of military family support is often on spouses and dependent children, the intergenerational influences of service extend much further. Military service shapes family dynamics across multiple generations in profound ways.

For "military brats" who grew up amid frequent relocations and a parent's deployments, these experiences indelibly shape their worldviews and self-concepts into adulthood. Studies show higher rates of emotional resilience and interpersonal adaptability in adults who moved frequently as military children; however, they also reveal greater difficulty developing long-term relationships and a persistent sense of rootlessness. Many feel drawn to careers or spouses connected to military service, continuing the family legacy.

Beyond children, the expectations and examples set by military parents and grandparents heavily influence descendants' values and life choices. Military service often becomes woven into the family identity across generations. Younger family members absorb passed-down traditions of duty, patriotism, courage, and sacrifice that guide their paths. Positive stories and memories of relatives' service inspire younger generations to pursue military careers.

But the generational impact extends beyond those who directly serve. Military family life inevitably involves loss and painful absences. When descendants observe the anguish of parents or grandparents missing in action or struggling with combat trauma, it often deters them from enlisting to spare family distress. Instead, they may honor relatives' sacrifices by supporting fellow veterans and military families through civilian service and activism.

Whether as a positive example or a cautionary tale, the ripple effects of ancestors' military service shape motivations, choices, and perspectives across generations. The unifying theme is service and sacrifice for a greater cause—a legacy passed down through families bound by military lives. Recognizing these lasting intergenerational influences provides a deeper understanding of military families' needs and experiences.

Part II
Time for Change

CHAPTER 6

Don't You Die on Me, Snodgrass!

On January 7, 2004, only 199 of us were in our seats by 0650 the next day; my fellow last-place finisher had washed out after the PT run with an injured ankle. We sat in hard metal folding chairs with integrated writing boards, no-nonsense and durable furniture, which, no doubt, someone in the U.S. Army Procurement Office calculated would last precisely 23.4 years.

The instructors advised us about customs, courtesies, and traditions in the military and the honors given to higher rank. "Your place of honor is on the right, subordination on the left, senior on the right. Respect all soldiers, and use military titles correctly. Use sir or ma'am to address the superiors." I took copious notes.

We learned about the proper numeral designations for rank. We were told to use professionalism in conversation and to always be formal and proper. When speaking with someone who had the same grade as us, we could use their first name, except in formal situations. We should remove our headgear indoors if we were unarmed. We must walk six steps behind the senior officer and always walk on the left of any superior officer. We were to use the greeting of the day and to honor the colors.

I learned that I should say, "Major Snodgrass reporting, Sir." And that you don't salute miniature flags. After traveling six paces (each pace the length of a human step) from the person you salute, you can drop your salute.

Finally, we were handed our class schedule for the next two days, with lectures to be shared by Captain Stern and Captain Al. Every salient point would need to be memorized.

We were told that the Army Reserve's medical strength was now 68 percent of what it had been five years earlier and that there were virtually no psychiatrists to be found anywhere within the Reserve. At that moment, it finally dawned on me: despite my pitiful physical condition, the Army would do anything and everything—literally whatever it takes—to get me through officer basic training. They desperately needed me, for I was a rare bird indeed.

On top of the physical stress, the emotional kind began to take its toll. On the night of Day 5, I stayed up studying until 2230 in my room before fatigue took over. Meanwhile, the majority of officer basic course (OBC) students were still studying on the fifth-floor lobby of Building 3084 well past midnight. By 1400 on the afternoon of January 8 (Day 5), I was done. I reported to sick call, where I was told to stay in bed for the rest of the day.

Later that evening, although I continued to feel mentally and physically exhausted and had serious problems concentrating, I knew I had to get ready for the quiz. Prompted by the sound of the steps of many fellow officers from the hallway outside who were still studying, I managed to pull myself out of bed. Down the hall was a lovely nurse with considerable experience and prior service time as a 91-Whiskey, 91W (health care specialist). At 2230 she joined me in the lobby, and we went over questions from a sample quiz. I returned to bed around 2300. I tried to call the operator for a wake-up call at 0400, but they were off-duty. My backup was the 91W. I went to tap on her door. She appeared in her nightgown and agreed to wake me at 0415. Back in my room, with my last ounce of strength, I finished packing my duffle for field training.

At 0415, I woke up with an uncomfortable feeling in my gut. I was weak, my head heavy, like it was caught in a hangover; I felt like death warmed over. As I finished prepping my gear for formation, I was numb and dazed, exhausted from a lack of restorative sleep and recovery and the anticipation of lining up in the field at 0445.

I should have listened to my gut. At 0500, in formation with trucks and troops and ready to receive orders, I discovered my MOPP (Mission Oriented Protective Posture) gear—for chemical, biological, radiological, nuclear toxic environments—was missing. I ran back to quarters and placed it in a small bag. When I returned and got back in line, my squad leader, who knew about my sick call, looked at me and asked, "How are you doing?"

"I would be doing better if I had another sick call day. I got no sleep last night."

"Neither did I," he said and briskly walked away.

Finally, our company commander barked from his megaphone, "NOW SOME OF YOU ARE DOCTORS, NURSES, LAB TECHNICIANS, BUT THAT DOESN'T COUNT NOW. THE ONLY THING YOU KNOW NOW IS THAT YOU ARE SOLDIERS. YOU REMEMBER THAT WHEN YOU GET OUT TO THE FIELD." Then came the merciless reminder of consequences: "AND IF ANY OF YOU REFUSE TO GO OUT TO THE FIELD, YOU WILL BE GOING STRAIGHT TO LEAVENWORTH."

During formation, several old buses had been waiting nearby with engines running and exhaust fumes coughing into the cold air of early dawn. Everything about this early morning assembly was surreal. It was before dawn, and I was still at a bare minimum level of vigilance for any spur-of-the-moment orders.

Once on the bus, I found my place next to my battle buddy (BB). I had hardly spoken to her during our first formation on January 6, that chilly morning on the second day of basic. She appeared disenchanted but withheld any utterances of disgruntlement. I now learnt that she was a second-year pathology resident at a hospital in Philadelphia and engaged. I was ambivalent about our pairing, it didn't help that she could run like a deer (aka run a seven-minute mile), which meant I had no chance of keeping up. During PT (physical training), we were in separate worlds. In not much time, however, our implicit mantra would become "toleration, cooperation." It had to be if we were going to make it through training together. During "honey bucket" (toilet) breaks in the field, we were coupled together, she waiting on me and vice versa.

My health was declining quickly. Based on my medical training, I diagnosed an onset of bronchitis. If I had expected the cold morning to evolve into a tolerable day, I was dead wrong; the desert became sweltering and humid during the afternoon exercise. I saw one of my comrades, a pharmacist, succumb to dehydration and collapse in the field, crumpling like a sick bird. We were strongly advised to drink water on a set schedule, whether we felt thirsty or not; Army rules for desert training mandated at least eight ounces of water every half hour. We were out in the field all day marching and learning about radio communications: how to send and receive messages, call in coordinates to avoid airstrikes in our area, and evacuate the wounded under combat operations.

At the end of the day, we made our way up a hill to an obstacle course, where we were to conduct an exercise with a "wounded" 150-pound mannequin resting on a litter. Our task was to hurdle a six-foot wall then grab it from the other side as two other grunts hoisted themselves over. The effort would be formidable. For one, the wall dwarfed my 5 foot 8 inch frame. And, to state the obvious, at 63, I was not the agile and nimble young man I once was.

First, I had to perform an overhead lift of my side of the litter and rest the handle on top of the wall. Then I had to leap high enough to grab a good chunk of the top of the wall and pull myself up and over it, a gymnastic challenge I probably would have struggled with in my 20s. Well, here goes nothing. I didn't come this far to cut and run.

Amazingly, I somehow made it to the top of the wall. My luck was tragically short-lived, however. I got stuck on top of the wall, with my legs dangling like a kicking frog.

Out of nowhere, I felt a hard push on my ass by the master sergeant (MSG). I looked around and saw him shaking his head. When we met the next day, he explained his motivations: "When I saw you go over that wall yesterday, I couldn't help thinking of my dad, how pitiful you looked." What could I say? He was probably right.

Following this obstacle feat, I was winded, lagging behind, and pale. Someone eyeballed me and told me to go to the first aid station—a makeshift, open-air covered bench. The medic looked at me and said to the sergeant, "This soldier is dehydrated." Then the med tech (who had just started training) began poking me to find a vein. After several fruitless attempts, I had had enough of this practice run. "This is not going to work!"

The noncommissioned officer supervisor agreed I had been tortured enough at the hands of the medic-in-training and ordered one of the sergeants to take me to the ER at the nearby Brooks Army Medical Center, where I was given an IV infusion of saline solution.

I knew precisely what was wrong with me, so I pleaded with the young doctor on duty, an intern who was clearly younger than 30, to give me some Zithromax, an antibiotic. He responded, "Oh if I did that, I would get into trouble. You don't have a fever."

The young doctor was adamant that I return to the field as soon as possible, informing me that the standard protocol was a return within 24 hours. I was discharged to quarters but without medicine. Army rules trump logic and, at times, even science.

My trip to the ER had at least one silver lining. It turned out that while I was lying in my hospital bed being fed IV fluids, my comrades were ushered into an auditorium that afternoon to listen to a lecture about the need to protect oneself against tear gas exposure. It turned out to be yet another Army ploy. With no advance warning and with no one having thought to bring their gas mask along to a lecture, the chamber was filled with a disabling tear gas. All 198 members of Alpha Company bolted from the room, coughing with tears streaming down their faces.

In so doing, and in its own inimitable way, the Army gave its recruits a realistic, though completely simulated, experience of chemical toxicity—a sort of indoctrination or training initiation for those who think war is purely theoretical. The tear gas wasn't harmful, but it had the instantaneous effect of infuriating my shocked colleagues while also making them realize that their instructors could not be fully trusted. More than one, I'm sure, suggested that the stunt was illegal, unethical, and potentially harmful. But after they calmed down and examined the incident more closely, they all seemed to take it in stride. The spontaneous gas attack was another example of how the Army does its best to prepare its people for the unexpected.

The MSG was at my barracks early the next morning for pick up—we would be returning to the training field. As he was rushing me back, I attempted to coax him to stop at a drugstore along the way so that I could prescribe myself the needed antibiotic. He flat-out refused. "We have to get back to the field. And besides, I don't see any drugstores here." No doubt he knew that bit of Army code that states, "Thou shalt not do anything without direct orders." Nowhere had anyone given him orders to drop me at a pharmacy, regardless of my age, health, rank, or anything else.

Alpha Company clapped in unison as I approached the inside of the large tent used as staff HQ, a huge morale booster for me. They were genuinely surprised to see me return, and I succeeded in absorbing some of their positive energy. I surmised that all my Alpha comrades expected me to have washed out. Esprit de corps is alive, and well, I thought.

When we got to the field, I walked over to a small hillside, bypassing the six-foot wall. I still had catch-up work to do. I sat on the hillside awaiting instructions, my M-16 and 9 mm Beretta by my side. My task was to pass a timed test evaluating how quickly I could clear a jammed gun (the M-16) in case I found myself in a firefight and needed to restore the weapon to functionality quickly. Then came the disassembling of the 9 mm, and then returning it to full operation, a two-minute time trial. I fumbled with the components, and with only 10 seconds left, the sergeant watching me with timer in hand looked dubious. And then, like magic, my piano fingers put all the Beretta parts perfectly together just as time ran out. I could scarcely believe my own eyes; I scored 15 out of 15 on the exercise. The sergeant looked amazed like he couldn't believe it either. I couldn't blame him.

I looked over and saw a group of grunts finishing their obstacle course runs. They were on a timed trial and were now crawling on their bellies under barbed wire while dragging that familiar 150-pound, sand-filled "patient" alongside them.

Out of sight, an NCO barked, "Snodgrass, get over here!" He had a roster in his hand with checkmarks across the page, signifying the successful completion of required exercises. He pointed to my name on the list. "It says here you haven't done the litter carry." I quickly replied, "I'm sick with bronchitis! I can't do it! Unless you have an easy one for me."

Oops. That seemed to catch his attention; it was as if a bolt of lightning went through his body. With a stern and intense gaze, he looked up from his clipboard and walked a step toward me, making some serious eye contact along the way.

"Easy?" he scoffed. "Is that what you said, soldier? Did you say *easy*?" His words hit me like a punch to the stomach. I realized I had said precisely the wrong words. At least, by that point, I knew it would be better to say nothing than to try to defend myself.

"Snodgrass, you get over there and do the litter carrying now. Your 24-hour sick call is over. They sent you back, and you are good to go."

I was incredulous. I had a compromised heart that skipped beats for up to 3.25 seconds at a time, and with my bronchial infection on top of that, I would really be pushing the envelope. One glance toward the platoon leader convinced me that this was a "take no prisoners" kind of situation. I was out of luck.

"Come on, Major, we'll help you do it," I heard the sergeant (who saw me straddle the wall the day before) say. I took no comfort in their words of encouragement. I knew the NCO's patience was on empty, and the sergeants were extremely eager to finish and get on with the day. (Later, when the ordeal was long over, I realized that they had literally done everything humanly and legally possible to get me to finish the obstacle course tasks, short of carrying my limp body around the training course.)

I had seen the detailed description of the litter carry in my textbook, but I hadn't realized the enormity of the challenge from the diagram. What seemed simple enough, in theory, required strength, stamina, coordination, and conditioning—all of which I lacked. The litter carry is meant to simulate the wheelless transport of wounded soldiers and is usually conducted over rough terrain. In real life, after giving first aid to a soldier, you would carry them on a litter to the closest available medical aid station.

Worse still, I soon discovered that my carry mandate was for not just one but four timed obstacle courses. I hid my internal gasp and dry mouth. With parched lips, I followed the MSG while being rushed down to a location with numerous stretchers lying on the turf. I was ordered to pick up one end of a stretcher while three other soldiers took their positions.

The other 198 recruits had all finished their litter carry exercise, so by default, my three "teammates" were all sergeant instructors—a fitter bunch of human beings you will never find. The hard part for me would not be carrying the weight; no, my hurdle would be merely keeping my grip on the litter while trying to keep pace with the rest of the group. The good news was that if I remained standing, the instructors would not let me fail. The bad news was that I was already gassed. One of the soldiers had the foresight to commemorate the historical moment with a photograph. Or maybe he wanted proof that if I keeled over, it was for the greater good. I could serve as an example of what the Army playbook expected for all the grunts, with no exceptions.

We began at a nearly jogging pace. "We gotta hurry! Move it!" shouted the first sergeant. The team lurched forward with massive acceleration, like a jet airplane taking off. It was all I could do to hang on for dear life. Three out of four courses crossed narrow bridges, natural and manmade barriers, and trenches. And all four had to be completed within the 15-minute time limit, or you had to do it again.

I began the obstacle course as a fourth stretcher bearer. Now, practically breathless and struggling for air, I was soon commanded to prepare for the two-man carry. Bearers two and three were going to change their holds on the litter handles to the other hand, step between hands, and take the full support of the litter, as bearers number one and four released their holds, a very tricky maneuver to execute if you have never done it before.

Now it was just me holding up the right rear carry while number one (left front) took the reins. He glanced at me over his shoulder with a disdainful look, gave a grunt, and then settled off at full speed through and over narrow passages and a series of culverts. The man was as strong as an ox, and I had no doubt that he could have levitated the entire litter from the front with no help from me whatsoever. At the precise moment we crossed the finish line, I fell and collapsed on the ground from exhaustion.

Then came the culmination, the final obstacle: a belly crawl under barbed wire while dragging the mannequin on a stretcher. I don't know how fast I was able to elevate my heart rate, but it was not accelerating normally to meet the challenge. The only thing they left out was the 50-caliber machine-gun bullets whizzing above my head. Well, I was still kicking, and I guess I was destined to pass the test.

By late afternoon, the command became concerned about my cardiovascular status. I again found myself at the first aid station. Like last time, I was exhausted, with shortness of breath and a tight chest. But now my entire body was vibrating with increasing pressure in my head. The medic performed a blood pressure check: 220/108, seriously bad.

The CO, Captain Jeff, came near, looked at my body lying supine, and said emphatically and with a bedside manner found only in the U.S. Army, "Major, now don't you die on me! Don't you die on me, Snodgrass!"

They strapped me to a gurney, and after several failed attempts at inserting an IV, a captain came over and swiftly performed it to perfection. I was rushed into an ambulance, ready to take me to my old stomping grounds, Brooks Army Medical Center. During the ride, I was monitored attentively by a paramedic. Lying on the floor of the ambulance, with careful eyes staring over me and an IV saline dripping into my veins, I could still feel the forceful pounding of each heartbeat, wondering if and when my blood pressure would stabilize. I knew a hypertensive crisis can damage blood vessels or potentially leak fluid or blood, and with my malfunctioning heart, I felt I was pushing against gravity. I was not looking forward to another trip to the ER. I kept my toes crossed, hoping I wouldn't encounter that same incompetent sophomore intern from the previous visit.

Following this second extended ER visit, which was primarily to evaluate and monitor my cardiovascular status and blood pressure and provide IV hydration, I was released again back to quarters. And this time, I was not released back to the field the next day.

Later that evening, hoping for a soft shoulder to cry on, I called my wife to complain about my brutal day. "I was so exhausted and wiped out that I could not walk up the hill to the next area where we were going to do biological warfare tactics. I mean, here I am, just trying to breathe. There's no mercy! No mercy! I'm way beyond that! I'm 63. There's no way I can fit into that mold. There's absolutely no way!"

And yet, in its incomparable and unsubtle way, the U.S. Army did precisely that—squeezing, prodding, poking, and pushing me, whenever necessary, to fit into an exact mold of its making, no matter how I felt about the one day of convalescence.

January 13, 2004: Day 10—Report to the Auditorium— The Laws of War

Another early morning rise and shine. Our company met at Blesse Auditorium at 0630, with lectures following at 0800 in Room 2004. Today we covered JAG stuff, including the Law of War, the Code of Conduct/Geneva Convention, standards of conduct, and military justice. I learned that according to the Geneva Convention, as a doctor, I must treat all patients according to the severity of their injuries. If several wounded soldiers come in at the same time, priority goes to the most severely injured, regardless of uniform, rank, nationality, or anything else. No one gets preferential treatment.

At 1330 hours, there was yet another meeting in Blesse Auditorium, and then we adjourned to Room 2305 at 1500 hours. In typical fashion, I tried my best to stay "alert."

With my head in the clouds, it finally happened: the D-word was spoken. Deployment. I could almost hear a pin drop when it was uttered. We were told by the LTC that there were only 12 thoracic surgeons in the entire Army medical corps before deployment, making them a very scarce—and high-demand—resource. We were also told that psychiatrists were on the hit list: 100 percent of them in last month's class were deployed from Fort Sam Houston, and 100 percent from this class would follow them to Iraq.

The LTC new about my sick sinus syndrome, and after class, she said that I had met my IMA (Individual Mobilization Augmentee) obligation for this year. As a result, I wouldn't have to go to the Army base in Heidelberg, Germany (where I'd train) until next year unless I decided differently. As an IMA soldier, I would be mobilized to support various commands and their areas of operation. This was usually a two-week period for all officers, and OBC would suffice for 2004. The annual requirement was to maintain readiness for active-duty orders; in my case, I would be preparing for eventual deployment.

She acknowledged that I was not fit for deployment to Iraq or any place without a general hospital. I felt considerably better after this conversation, mostly because I realized that the U.S. Army was indeed looking out for my welfare. There was no malintent whatsoever there.

However, during my first mobilization to active duty that same year, I learned of the Army's urgent need for someone with my skills to serve in Iraq, and I would again be screened and encouraged to fill that vacuum. It was a persuasive screening maneuver to try to add me to that very thin and depleted line of psychiatrists who were needed in Iraq.

After class, soldiers with worrisome faces sidled up to me and introduced themselves. Apparently, word had gotten around that I was a trained psychiatrist and that I might be of some help to members of Alpha Company. I had to give some counseling and therapy on the spot, including to a tall, handsome young radiologist who was extremely anxious about his status. "Major Snodgrass, you seem to be quite calm about things," he said. I listened to his concerns and angst about his impending deployment. The impromptu 10-minute psychotherapy session appeared to put him at greater ease. I listened empathically to the pulse of his emotions, and with sincere conviction, I attempted to reassure him that the Army would promote the proper care, welfare, and safety of their doctors (like him) in the medical corps no matter where they were posted.

The next-oldest doctor, Dr. S., was standing nearby and also looked anxious, and understandably so, as he was about to be deployed as well. He was a 52-year-old orthopedic surgeon from Idaho. "Hey, I would have been sent to Iraq last month if I had come to OBC in December," he said, perhaps coming to appreciate the fact that, a few weeks later, he was still stateside and safe.

Then a captain started to tell me his own tale of woe, about his girlfriend of the past few months who was unsure about keeping a relationship with him. She lived in Florida; he lived in Michigan. Her parents recently divorced, and she was very distraught and insecure about what she considered a betrayal of trust. She feared that all of her significant others would eventually leave her as well. The captain had just been informed that he would be deployed to Iraq, and he was deeply worried. He did not know how to break the news to her in a way that wouldn't make her feel devastated or abandoned. I offered him what the Army calls directive counseling. I advised him first to call her and, second, to promise to see her within the next two weeks—in fact, they should try to get away for a long weekend. He smiled and said, "You're right. Thank you." He then turned to another subject that had been pressing on his mind, namely the Army mentality. "I don't feel I belong here," he admitted. "Everyone is doing what they're doing just because they have someone giving them orders."

"Yes, that's right. You and I made it through medical school because of intrinsic motivation."

He interrupted. "That's it! That's an excellent word. I have been trying to describe this. You're right. We didn't have someone giving us orders to study. We did this on our own with no one looking on."

We shared our mutual disdain for how certain aspects of the Army's way of life ran counter to our emotions and perception of ourselves as physicians. The truth is that everyone in the Army complains about the Army nearly all the time. But at the same time, no one has yet been able to come up with a better system or organization that can quickly mold civilians into combat-ready troops. He shook my hand and smiled. As we departed, he promised to follow up with me by email, but I never heard from him again.

The final meeting of the afternoon, at 1500, was opened by an introduction from a female colonel with gray hair who looked somewhat like my Grandma Fink when she was in her 70s. This colonel had recently returned from Afghanistan, where she had been assigned for 90 days, quickly explained that the 90-day "boots on the ground" policy usually meant 120 days in real time, taking into account in-processing and out-processing and available flights from the warzone. Considering that she had just come from said warzone, we were expecting to hear a riveting story of her duties as an Army physician assigned to such a harsh and hostile environment.

Unfortunately, the colonel had absolutely no personality and offered no inspiration for us soon-to-be graduates to use. Her delivery had all the excitement of watching paint dry, and the content felt like it had come directly from an instructor's manual. The assembly finally broke up after numerous one-to-one short queries with the AMEDD (Army Medical Department) staff, who made themselves available for questions afterward.

My comrades and I walked back to the dining hall for a warm meal. At the beginning of basic training, I looked forward to these meals, but as days went on, they gradually lost their luster with the lack of changes or variety. The soft ice cream was usually a temptation, and of course, their price of $3.30 for a full dinner was a bargain. No argument there.

On my trips to the dining hall, I would often find myself returning salutes multiple times to all of the young recruits (juniors to me), especially as I held the rank of major. Gazing upon those innocent faces of the 18- and 19-year-olds who never knew the stark reality of the call "to be all that you can be" was at times shocking; they appeared as mere children to this senior adult of 63 years. They were always mindful of respect, even in the dining hall, when the hat salute was on pause mode. They would address me as "Sir."

The evening after the colonel's uninspiring lecture, any free time after dinner was to be for studying. I wanted to let it slide, but of course, duty would not allow me. Our last exam was in the morning at 0730, and Lieutenant Jasmine, whose room was down the hall from my fifth-floor accommodation, invited me to drop in for a review of our study material. But first, adding to our toils, we had to make sure we organized our field gear, which was to be turned in to the CIF (Central Issue Facility) at noon the next day. All of these combat field accouterments were supposed to be cleaned, but I quickly ran into trouble. How do you clean a sleeping bag? I sure didn't know. Lieutenant Jasmine gave me some advice on how to rearrange all my gear so that it could be repacked into the duffel bag in the correct sequence. (I found out later that the sequence would be changed once we arrived at CIF for out-processing. Oh well; it sounded good at the time.) Back in my room, I sorted out my gear, canteens, ground cloth, poncho, ammunition, pouches, compass, pills pouch, mop gear with gas mask, and did some cleaning. It was getting on toward 2100 by the time we were finished with this exercise plus a brief review of test materials. I needed to return all my gear back to my room, but I accepted Jasmine's offer for a sample quiz later that night.

Upon my return to Jasmine's room, we were joined by a young soldier who stood at an ironing board pressing his uniform for the next day's dress rehearsal graduation. Jasmine appeared preoccupied and pensive like something had come up, but her willingness to help me hadn't changed. She calculated that, based on my previous exam scores and my performance with the radio, M-16, 9 mm, litter carry, and grappling under the barbed wire, I would only need to pass half of the test questions to graduate from OBC. This was a relief to hear, as I did not have much motivation to study seriously. I was fatigued, and I did not have a good feeling about this exam.

The residual effects of the upper respiratory infection, plus the lack of sleep, had worn me down and depleted my energy. Jasmine inferred that I would be invited to graduation rehearsal the next day, a premature but hopeful sign, provided I could manage a pass on the final. The prospect of failing made me think about my health issues and the botched attempts to remain in the field. A failure would mandate a repeat of OBC within six months. At that moment, I could not fathom anything more humiliating. Yes, the sergeants' motto was, "It's all good." But mine was, "All's well that ends well."

Upon returning to my room, I took an over-the-counter cold and flu tablet, which had an antihistamine, and proceeded to do my own review out of sheer duty or anxiety. Drowsiness overtook me, and I soon closed the book and turned out the lights.

The following day, January 14, I received the final exam wake-up call at 0600. I used the coffeemaker to produce some weak pearl jasmine tea and munched on the last of the granola bars for my breakfast. I arrived at Room 2404, where at precisely 0730, the instructor handed out test booklets and answer sheets. I was the last person to leave the classroom; as I exited, the instructor said, "Tell them all to come back in." I thought to myself that this was a good sign; the assistant for assignment indicated that she wanted me to be seen by my peers as the last to walk out of the classroom. By my lights, she wouldn't ask someone who had failed to do this. Right?

We assembled and waited for our papers to be returned and scored. I saw mine, quickly grabbed it, and turned it over so others couldn't see my score: 17 out of 25—one point below passing. As luck would have it, however, one of the test questions was thrown out because it was not on the yellow list (a set of questions that counted toward the net threshold for a pass). In the end, I received an 18, a barely passing score.

I was feeling down all morning. To help take my mind off the stupid test, I paid a visit to the Army Medic Museum from 0930 to 1020. This genuinely enlightening, thought-provoking institution chronicles the history of the Medical Services Corps in the Army from 1775 to the present and wonderfully portrays the selfless dedication of those nurses, medics, and doctors who served in their finest hour under heavy combat. A little later in the day, the museum was going to show a two-hour film about POW trauma, but I didn't have enough time to catch it. I took many photos, though, of the history on display.

The entire exam process was still on my mind. I wondered about what it must have been like for the 50 poor soldiers who failed the first test during the first day in the field and were counseled by Captain Jeff until 0130 the next morning. Command got them out of bed in the middle of the night and brought them to his tent for counsel.

Well, that didn't happen to me. And I was cautiously optimistic that I was probably going to graduate that day. I hoped that my pass on the final exam, along with my other scores, would be enough to squeeze a pass for OBC. My gut quivered a bit. But before I could feel even sorrier for myself, first I had to do my out-processing at the CIF.

On the way over, I made a pit stop at the latrine. After the much-needed relief, I accidentally dropped my cap on the floor just beneath the urinal. Even after thinking about all of those who had left their golden drops on the floor before me, I impulsively grabbed my hat, placed it on my head, and headed out the door. In less than two weeks, the Army had extinguished my germaphobia and, in its place, instilled a ruthless pragmatism.

Hurry up and wait. My fellow squad members and I arrived at the CIF as ordered at 1145, but the doors were locked. Then, after a long time standing around, we were told that we would be among the last platoon to be processed. This meant about another two-hour wait. In the meantime, we made the trek back to AMEDD briefly to return the gas mask. While I was waiting in line to hear my name called, my battle buddy, Vickie, came up to me and said, "Let me see what size your mask is." I knew that I had checked out a size medium. To my amazement, someone had switched things up on me—I was holding a size large. "This is why I couldn't get a good seal on my mask."

"Yeah. Someone stole my small mask, and I believe I have a medium to exchange with you," said Vicki. What luck. So now we could return the rightful property without reprimand. But who steals a mask in the first place?

As we were standing in line at out-processing, all holding our battle gear and duffel bags, we got word of the two written test score averages for the four platoons. We, the fourth platoon, had been in first place, but after the second test score was added in, we dropped to second. I gazed around sheepishly, convinced I had been our platoon's spoiled apple. Of course, I couldn't prove it.

Graduation commenced at 1600 hours. All rose to face the flag, as a soldier no one could identify but sang a moving rendition of the "Star-Spangled Banner." Then the chaplain gave the convocation, and all heads bowed. In his prayer, he called on God to keep safe those of us who would be going to Iraq and placed in harm's way.

Then came the acknowledgment of the highest physical training test scores. My battle buddy was second highest for points with 290; mine was a meager 150.

Next up was our guest speaker, Lieutenant Colonel Brown, a Johns Hopkins Medical School graduate with a specialty in thoracic surgery. I was really hoping it would be an uplifting and memorable speech, but not a chance. Eye contact with the audience—practically nil. No intimacy with the listeners. And he read every word of this non-inspiring address. But after all, who in the heck cares? This was our time to feel relieved. We had made graduation. Our names were on the certificates. We were soldiers.

In celebration, it was time to go over financial reimbursement forms and wait in even more long lines to tie up various bureaucratic loose ends. Finally, after an agonizing two hours of this chaos, we returned to BOQ (bachelor officer quarters) for hot showers. It was like a cleansing of all the ugly unpleasantries of basic training.

A trio consisting of me, a friendly med-tech lieutenant named George, and Vickie met in the lobby at 1900 hours to go to the graduation party being held at the NCO club reserved just for us officers. We decided to walk, lest there be any chance of being picked up for DUI upon our return from the bash. Although we had only known each other for less than two weeks, the intensity of the training sessions made all of us in Alpha Company quick friends. In the few minutes we had to socialize outside of class I felt a sense of acceptance and unity. Through the collective effort for completion of a major task I was able to share with pride, the comradery and immediate bonding with my fellow members of Alpha Company. They were all men and women who had previously served and could have easily avoided this new round of military service had they so chosen. These were all "special people," I told my wife, Tong, later that evening in a phone call, with more than a touch of admiration. We connected in shared misery, suffering, sacrifice, and a common goal to serve our country with honor. Indeed, I could not have been prouder to be a member of Alpha Company. Despite my declining health and the hardships and stress I was forced to endure, as I signed off my call that evening, I still managed to look at the experience as being incredibly positive. "I'm a lucky guy," I told Tong.

An interesting anecdote I heard that last night: one of my comrades, Major Sulley, was newly married, and her husband, also serving in the Army, had just received orders to deploy to Iraq in two days. The evening of the party, she waited in her room for his call. He said he would be able to see her, but just for one hour, and only if she could fly to New Jersey and come to his unit in her BDU (Battle Dress Uniform, i.e., camouflaged combat uniform) to appear official. Without hesitation, the next day (Friday), she purchased a ticket to fly five and a half hours to Manchester, New Jersey, home to Fort Dix, the joint training site for all branches of the service. This story was yet another reminder that few of us ever know or appreciate some of the enormous sacrifices our fine members of the armed services make to serve America while simultaneously balancing relationships with their families. Freedom is not free. It always extracts a price of selfless sacrifice.

Graduating was nothing short of miraculous. I had barely earned the required number of points but somehow, in some way, squeezed through. The last thing I wanted was to return to San Antonio to repeat basic in six months. Despite my discomfiting low score, there are very few accomplishments in my life of which I am prouder. As I made my way through those 12 grueling days, my load was lessened by the genuine, unmistakable sincerity and dedication of my fellow recruits. On top of that, I was one of only two Whiskey 60s (Army alphabet, W-60 designated for psychiatrists) in our company. The other one was approximately 30 years my junior.

The celebration on graduation day, January 16, was all too brief; there was much more we could have shared in our frenzy that day. My first blush of military bearing aroused in me a new and fresh look at patriotism. I had transcended into a gestalt, a force greater than the sum of its members. In the end, we were all battle buddies for a common cause.

I understand now that the hardship, pain, stress, 18-hour days, physical and emotional abuse, not to mention inedible food and bare-bones accommodations, all served their purpose—I became tougher, more resilient, more impervious to criticism, and at the same time, deeply bonded to my fellow soldiers. These are people for whom I would literally have given my own life to save. Basic training had leveled the playing field. We were all the same, just grunts in the desert field, regardless of rank. This was a ground-zero experience for erasing socioeconomic and cultural differences. What other two-week training courses could accomplish such admirable goals?

As harsh as my course of training was—and despite the lack of empathy and assistance I received from many of my instructors and commanding officers—if I had been put in charge of the whole operation, I can honestly say I would do it all exactly the same way, with one minor exception. Perhaps the Army doctors could have ascribed some value to my 30-plus years of medical training when it came to determining my best course of treatment in those hospital visits.

That said, while I still believe that the Army could have easily prescribed an antibiotic a couple of days sooner, which might have alleviated some of my sufferings, I bear absolutely no malice or resentment toward them. The eminence of the U.S. Army is supposed to be without question.

The slogan for the 187th Alpha Company was "Hardcore, med core, hoorah!" At the graduation ceremony, I was able to stand and say

"Hoorah!" and actually realize what it meant. Up to that point in my life, the power contained in such a cheer had been utterly foreign to me.

I knew the challenge for me to be seen as worthy of the battle duty uniform which I wore would be formidable. As a senior with no military experience, I felt the weight of responsibility and honor that comes with donning such a symbol of service and sacrifice. I had to demonstrate commitment and dedication to the values and ideals that the uniform represented. While I did not have the experience or training of the members of Alpha Company, I was determined to show that I possessed the qualities of discipline, integrity, and resilience that are essential and strive to embody the ethos of the uniform. In the end I understood that proving myself worthy of wearing it was not about comparing myself to others, but rather about exhibiting the qualities of character and fortitude that it symbolized. I may have started with doubt and uncertainty, but I left with a profound sense of pride, knowing that I earned the privilege of wearing it.

Passing any version of basic training for the first time at 63, making me likely the oldest person ever to do so, was only the first major obstacle in my delayed military career. My first deployment lay ahead of me. But I would soon discover that the Army had, perhaps by design, turned me into a new man.

The Army needed me, and the Army got me through. Recruiting numbers are down. There are others out there like me who could help fill the vacancies if given a chance. Welcoming seniors into the military service can strengthen the cohesion and diversity within a unit and encourage a shared commitment to serving the country. This fosters a collaboration for mutual support and respect.

CHAPTER 7

Reimagining Age Limits for Military Service

Surgeon. Crile Doscher, who served active duty two years during the Vietnam War, said in a 2023 interview:

> I think that if World War III comes along, which it might because they're choosing up sides already, I will be the first in line to volunteer. And I say that sincerely. I'm 88, but I don't care how old we are. There's always something we can do that is productive. And don't think that age leaves you incompetent to the point where you cannot do something productive for your country, even if it's triage. You know, in our profession, yours and mine, we could triage patients. I probably couldn't do productive surgery because I've been out of it too long but damned if I couldn't do triage quite well and act as a personal assistant in the operating room or something of that magnitude. And I would do that. I'd be first in line tomorrow morning.

Equally convincing is an interview in 2023, with 30-year veteran, Colonel Strones, only two months shy of his 82nd birthday, who asserted, "If they gave me a chance, I would join up now."

Even if World War III were to happen, it remains doubtful that any military organization would allow an 82- or 88-year-old to be on active duty in any capacity, whether on U.S. soil or elsewhere. And yet, there are compelling reasons why such an idea should be considered and made a permanent fixture of how military organizations recruit.

Take me as a case in point. I chose to join the Army as a 63-year-old, a decision I remain immensely proud of to this day. Reflecting on my journey, the pivotal year of 1991 was the crucible that tested my dedication and drew on years of experience that I simply would not have had at my disposal as a younger recruit.

At the time, I was living in Nuremberg, Germany, working as the in-patient psychiatry service chief at the 98th General Army Hospital. A steady stream of Gulf War casualties poured in, those both physically and mentally scarred. One such patient was a young *Desert Storm* veteran, a man we'll refer to as NB. His diagnosis was organic brain syndrome and delirium, a complex condition that would soon entangle his case with my own in a convoluted web.

On top of his complex medical needs, he was being questioned by the Criminal Investigation Division (CID) regarding the alleged shooting of Iraqi POWs, an allegation he repeatedly denied. As an experienced practitioner, it was clear to me that his already fragile mental state was deteriorating further under their harsh spotlight. And on top of that, one of the CID agents continued to press me about whether NB had divulged anything regarding the allegations. I held firm, staunchly asserting the sacrosanct importance of patient confidentiality. I did not bend to the pressure, even when my apartment was raided for evidence.

I stuck to the mantra "age imparts wisdom." The tempting path of least resistance—capitulating, following protocol, not rocking the boat—may have appealed to a younger physician lacking my commitment, but, seasoned by decades of experience, I knew that maintaining my patients' trust outweighed all else.

With pressure building from the CID, and my patient's mental state continuing to deteriorate, I knew I needed to dig deep and draw on any reserves I could muster. Once again, I hearkened back to the Hippocratic oath (Do no harm!) and refused to compromise my principles.

Fortunately, my integrity stayed intact, as an American attorney based in Germany learned of my predicament and validated my unwavering stance on upholding patient confidentiality, assuring me that my legal footing was solid. His stern letter to the Army High Command forcefully asserting my innocence helped calm the raging storm around me.

In due course, NB was eventually transferred back to the States for further treatment, though his ultimate fate remained obscured to me. I took solace in knowing that he had at least managed to evade the Army's clutches for a military trial based on unproven war crime accusations. Whether NB was truly innocent or had simply been too mentally incapacitated to grasp the gravity of his alleged actions, I may never know for certain.

During this harrowing episode, my age became a kind of armor. The accumulated decades of living and learning had taught me how to sustain resilience and maintain moral courage when tested. At an age when most officers would have gladly hung up their boots, I stood firm. Moral courage and wisdom should be respected as much as blind obedience up the chain of command.

I never saw my journey as a spiteful battle against the Army itself. Instead, it was a struggle to make the organization stronger, more moral, and more humane in dealing with vulnerable soldiers like NB. I consider myself a patriot, and my allegiance to the Army and my country remains unbroken. As I navigated the choppy waters of this dispute, I nurtured a hope that my small stand could perhaps chart a course for a future where true justice and compassion are no longer mutually exclusive—where moral courage and wisdom are respected as much as blind obedience up the chain of command. In the end, I am genuinely grateful for that formative experience. It shaped me into who I am today, revealing unknown parts of my character. It taught me viscerally about the formidable power of unflinching integrity, no matter the forces allied against you. I learned that moral courage matters just as much as physical bravery, especially in the Army.

It's Time for Change

The status quo of arbitrary age restrictions makes little sense in modern times. On the front end, we are sending many teens into service who lack the maturity and resilience to handle the demands. We have already discussed how the fallout in terms of PTSD, depression, and suicide can take a tragic toll. At the same time, older professionals with extensive expertise are excluded due to outdated notions of aging. We ignore their potential contributions at society's peril.

One potential policy update to consider is raising the minimum enlistment age to 21 for combat roles while still providing non-combat positions better suited for 18–20-year-olds. Additionally, more rigorous psychological screening before enlistment could help assess maturity, resilience, motivations, and family background to determine who is truly ready for the demands of service. Providing alternative paths to college besides military service, such as making community college and vocational training more affordable, would also give young people looking to further their education more options besides just enlisting.

Once in the military, expanding mental health resources for active-duty personnel and veterans, and breaking the stigma around seeking care, could help identify and treat those struggling with the psychological toll. We need to continue to train officers to recognize mental health issues early and intervene appropriately, rather than just removing their stripes or discharging them. We have made some progress but there is still more to be done. Incorporating trauma-informed care principles into training and leadership practices and understanding the profound impacts trauma can have on development would likewise lead to policies and programs better suited to young recruits.

We should remove blanket age barriers for older citizens and evaluate competence individually per role. We can strengthen America's armed forces responsibly and humanely with care and open minds.

But change will only occur through public awareness and debate. Neither strictly limiting nor blindly expanding the age range will work in isolation. What matters most is upholding the humanity and dignity of every recruit, guiding them to serve in a way that nurtures their talents. The time has come to chart a wiser course.

Military Culture and Aging

The military is deeply rooted in an established culture that values discipline, physical fitness, and readiness for combat. Within this framework, including older individuals may present challenges in meeting rigorous physical demands and potential resistance to change within a traditionally youth-oriented environment. However, military culture also places a high premium on experience, adaptability, leadership, and resilience, often recognizing the value that older generations can bring.

One significant advantage of having an older military force is their wealth of life experience and wisdom. Over years of service and exposure to various situations, more senior military personnel can bring unique perspectives, enhanced problem-solving abilities, and invaluable mentorship to younger troops. The wisdom gained from prior deployments, combined with an enhanced ability to assess risks and make informed decisions, can significantly contribute to the overall effectiveness of the force.

Exploring the advantages of an older military force requires consideration of career advancement. Establishing straightforward paths for promotion, growth, and acknowledgment can aid senior staff in maintaining their valuable knowledge, skills, and accumulated experience. Initiatives like mentorship programs and leadership development opportunities can harness their specialized expertise and skill sets, fostering a climate of continued commitment and inspiration for the younger generation in the military.

The rapid advancement of technology also offsets some of the traditionally stringent physical mandates and requirements. It opens a gateway for seniors wanting to join the ranks and begin a new career. For example, many retired doctors have hired on with the VA to extend their practice and share their valuable skills and experience, a valuable resource for VA medical centers across the U.S. and foreseeably for other institutions. This untapped resource has existed for years, but military regulations and arbitrary mandates have prevented access to such senior personnel. These 60–70-year-olds do not require a PT run or need to prove their prowess with push-ups. Their minds are sharp, and many can still hold steady a scalpel. The VA has made flexible regulations so that many elderly physicians can see patients via virtual media. Not having to travel lightens the workload of physical demands for providers and decreases the "no-shows" on follow-up visits.

One undeniable truth often emerges in pursuing exceptional medical expertise: age is not synonymous with diminished skill or competence. The notion that outstanding doctors over the age of 60 and even 70 possess formidable skills and an unparalleled wealth of experience is widely acknowledged. Their extensive knowledge, refined expertise, and proven track record testify to their invaluable contributions to the medical field.

However, it is perplexing that the same degree of value and recognition is not extended to these professionals within military contexts. One might question why the military holds reservations about welcoming physicians who possess the aptitude to serve dutifully and proficiently. Considering the rigorous demands placed upon medical professionals in military settings, the indomitable skills that doctors over 60 possess should be harnessed to optimize patient care and augment the capability of the medical corps, often understaffed.

The decision to overlook this ignored resource is a critical mistake. Higher echelons in the military must recognize that age should never be the sole determinant for evaluating one's ability to contribute effectively. The collective wisdom of senior doctors over 60 or even 70 could significantly enhance the delivery of medical services in the military.

To address this discrepancy, it is time for the military to reevaluate and reframe their perspective, granting due recognition and value to the capabilities and contributions of senior doctors and other medical specialists, such as therapists, psychologists, and nurse specialists. By doing so, we can bridge the gap between the wealth of experience these professionals bring and the need for skilled medical personnel in demanding military environments.

The Army does occasionally grant age waivers and often allows veterans (who served at a younger age) the opportunity to serve as practicing physicians. In this process, the Army subtracts one's prior duty time, e.g., five years, from their current calendar age. The math does the rest; thus, they fall below the maximum entry age. For the older non-veterans, the Army has adopted a program called OAPP (Officer Accession Pilot Program), which offers an opportunity for practicing physicians aged 43–60 years to serve for a period of two years.

Such was the case for 61-year-old JM, who joined in 2013 and headed off to officer basic training at Fort Sam Houston, Camp Bullis, where he had communication training and learned how to evacuate casualties under strenuous conditions. Such training could be difficult for even today's young soldiers. He had experienced Army basic training 30 years before. At age 61, he had to pass the officer basic training before being given his active-duty assignment. After graduation from basic training, he requested deployment to Afghanistan and was placed on an alternate deployment list due to his age (*Army Medicine*, January 29, 2013, "61-year-old joins the Army, hopes to follow in father's footsteps").

A critical shortage has been developing for the past several years (since 2011) for health care in the military, with fewer doctors in uniform. Vital to this concern has been the military's inability to recruit and retain a sufficient number of doctors. Even under normal conditions, without the COVID-19 pandemic, the military was struggling to handle the patient case workload and have since shifted the burdensome caseload to the civilian community to manage their shortage of doctors of various specialties. Ironically, the budget for military health has been diminishing since its peak in 2011. Even the Department of Defense has proposed eliminating 15,000 military doctors and nurses (*USA Today*, July 18, 2019, "US Doctor Shortage: Pentagon plans unwise cuts in military doctors").

The argument against allowing those over age 40 to enter military service for the first time is that, as a group, they are less physically fit for military duty. This statement may be accurate, but there is much to be said about acquiring invaluable skills and experience that can provide a wealth of resources, especially in health care. With such a dire need for doctors and other medical specialists in the military, it is time to rethink the rationale of archaic rules.

As a case in point, I was deployed overseas at age 68 in 2008. Near the end of my deployment, there were military clinics without a physician with my specialty (psychiatry). I requested to extend my active-duty obligation to two more years so that I could volunteer to fill one of those vacancies. A letter of denial came back from Army headquarters. The reason given was that I had no prior military service. I looked for support from a two-star general, but to no avail. She stated, "It would take an act of Congress."

It seemed like a no-brainer. Why would a practicing doctor with valuable clinical experience, available to fill a vital key medical position in a time of war, be denied due to arbitrary regulation based on not having served in the military at an earlier age? Looking through another lens, I guess I was lucky to have served. My entrance into the military was short of a miracle and required support from pay grades beyond colonel and superior arm twisting at the Pentagon. However, there is a glaring double standard when it comes to politics and military age standards—no upper age limit for running for president, commander in chief. By rule, a presidential candidate must be at least 35 years of age and a citizen, residing in the U.S. for 14 years.

Many older physicians beyond their 60s who are not veterans have a burning desire to serve and would grab the chance to join the ranks of the military medical corps. In addition, there are thousands of doctors over 60 who, if they had a chance, would give up their practices or come out of retirement to enter military service.

JM referred to his move from private practice to the military as an opportune experience to retire and find a new challenge. The military offers a grand stage, a platform for selfless service with honor, a cherished history of sacrifice, and a duty to care for those who have borne the wounds and scars of service and those who continue to serve active duty.

Rethinking Physical Fitness Standards

Much emphasis gets placed on physical fitness tests as a requirement for military service. While strength and endurance are valuable assets, the current fitness benchmarks fail to account for other attributes that contribute to success. Resilience, adaptability, emotional maturity, cognitive abilities, and life experience also play essential roles.

Take the Army Physical Fitness Test (APFT), for example. It consists of timed push-ups, sit-ups, and a two-mile run. Performance on these measures tends to decline with age. So it is assumed that older recruits would do poorer on the APFT overall. However, these standardized tests offer limited insight into real-world capabilities. Older officer candidates may not run as fast but have greater endurance at a lower speed gained from years of physical activity. Their strength comes from wisdom and composure under stress versus brute force alone.

We must expand our concept of readiness beyond arbitrary fitness benchmarks. An experienced 60-year-old doctor will perform surgery better than a 22-year-old athlete. Special Forces select candidates based on critical thinking, teamwork, and specialized skills—not just push-up prowess. Likewise, the military should consider placing more value on knowledge, cognitive abilities, expertise, education, psychological resilience, leadership qualities, and training aptitude when determining one's "fitness" for duty.

If the work involved does not require marching into combat zones, why impose narrow physical standards on those with valuable capabilities? There are many essential military jobs, such as medical care and strategic advising, that could be performed effectively by those who may not pass rigid fitness tests. With flexible policies focusing on individual strengths and job requirements, the young and old can better serve America's defense.

The Multifaceted Benefits of Welcoming Older Recruits

Allowing qualified older individuals to join or reenter military service would infuse critical diversity of experience into the armed forces. Older recruits bring worldviews shaped by decades of education, work, setbacks, achievements, and relationships. Their varied perspectives derived from living full lives provide nuance and balance to complement younger enlisted members' worldviews. Over time, they also accumulate specialized skills and niche expertise that are invaluable assets—foreign languages, cybersecurity, aeronautics, law, psychology, and countless other fields. The military spends tremendous resources training recruits in these disciplines from scratch when older candidates already possess them. Eliminating age restrictions can allow the military to benefit from these recruits' rich experience and talents honed over long careers.

Older individuals can also help address the military's recruitment challenges through multiple avenues. First, simply expanding age eligibility spontaneously grows the pool of potential recruits the military can draw from. With shifting demographics that shrink the population of eligible young people, discarding arbitrary age limits is a pragmatic necessity. Second, while not all roles demand peak physical fitness, older recruits can still effectively serve in positions matched to their capabilities—as instructors, analysts, technical specialists, administrators, trainers, and advisors. Their contributions to these non-combat roles could enhance the military's overall mission. Third, allowing veterans to return to duty retains years of invaluable operational knowledge and helps experienced soldiers mentor the next generation. Younger recruits can benefit tremendously from learning alongside seasoned veterans. And fourth, welcoming older recruits signals a message of meritocracy and inclusivity that can strengthen the military's culture. An age-diverse force aligned with modern society projects an image of transparency, fairness, and opportunity—one where commitment and competence matter more than age.

Older individuals' talents and competencies also align well with the armed forces' evolving needs in a changing world. As technology permeates the battlefield, recruits with backgrounds in technical fields like cybersecurity or aerospace engineering lend crucial expertise that the military desperately requires. Others bring knowledge gained from civilian sector careers in law, medicine, psychology, and business that directly apply to military functions like legal advising, health care administration, human resources, and financial management. Still others offer language skills and cultural knowledge imperative for diplomatic engagements and peacekeeping missions abroad. With dynamic threats and increasing complexity, the military needs recruits with multifaceted experiences—exactly what older candidates poised for second careers possess.

Finally, discarding arbitrary age restrictions fully lives up to the military's democratic ideals. Institutional discrimination that precludes older recruits contradicts principles of equal opportunity. All those with the capability, will, and character to serve their nation should have the chance to demonstrate their abilities, whatever their age. The armed forces' greatness lies in motivated Americans from all walks of life dedicated to a higher purpose. An intergenerational force that embraces and leverages the diverse strengths of all qualified demographics keeps the military aligned with modern society's expectations and diversity. By upholding these democratic values, the armed forces can continue evolving as an elite yet inclusive institution prepared to face any challenge.

If nothing else, the above points argue that it is time for a reexamination of the reasons why arbitrary age limits are placed on those who wish to serve. If the reason why countries have military organizations, to begin with, is to protect the civilian population, on what basis does it make sense to exclude millions of qualified individuals who could contribute mightily to the cause?

Crusty Old Soldiers

Our historical view of the senior military (officers and NCOs) is a tough 45–55-year-old. They display a chest full of medals, and command brigades or larger units. They are the acknowledged "experts" in their fields, combat units, or the more plentiful support units. The latter comprise many more soldiers of equal seniority.

These constitute a vast pool of soldiers with equal military schooling, experience, and knowledge. These people provide an extensive reservoir of skill in the various areas needed to support a division or army at war. Unfortunately, these are also the persons most likely to be retired as they are "too old" or to make room to promote the next generation of officers.

Compare this with a large American corporation comprising several presidents or managers of each major division (manufacturing, sales, research, energy, finance, and more). Within those divisions might be several vice presidents, and below those is a range of personnel who comprise the "working knowledge" or expertise of that company. Their skill set is comparable to the senior staff in a military division. These are the ones counted on to respond to a crisis. The primary difference, perhaps, is that corporations value these senior persons even if they may be unable to run a mile, are overweight, unable to relocate, or are fighting chronic disease. Remember that in a time of war, those soldiers scheduled for retirement or recently retired may have separation orders put on hold or be called back to active duty. Persons with special skills (e.g., specific medical or technical abilities) may also be allowed to enter the Army despite violating sacrosanct age requirements.

In my case, I joined the Army at age 60+ because my psychiatric experience was desperately needed due to the Army at war in Iraq.

124 • THE AGELESS CALL TO SERVE

I was the only 60-W (psychiatrist) save one in our entire company. Having been turned down after my swear-in due to age, I persevered despite the odds and finally, three years later, was granted an almost miraculous exception.

These relatively senior corporate members provide a pool of unique knowledge processes and corporate culture and serve as mentors for new hires. As a result, corporations encourage them to stay. Yet, despite the above, the Army lets them go.

There are a few exceptions. For example, naval admirals are the most senior officers in any navy worldwide. Though it is a physically demanding and high-pressure job, a few outstanding individuals have managed to retire at 80 or more.

Five of the best admirals who retired after 80 are four-star Admiral Arleigh Burke, known for his innovative naval tactics and help with the missile programs. Even after retirement, he continued to advise the U.S. government on naval issues until his death at age 94. Four-star Admiral Ernest King executed naval campaigns against Germany and Japan during World War II and remained active in maritime affairs until his death at 82. Chester Nimitz, following World War II, retired at age 76 but continued to be involved in naval affairs until his death at 80. Hyman Rickover, a four-star admiral regarded as the "Father of the Nuclear Navy," retired at 82 and remained active in naval affairs until his death at 86. Finally, five-star Admiral Ram Dass Katari served as Chief of the Naval Staff of the Indian Navy from 1984 to 1987. He was crucial in modernizing the Indian Navy and was vital to developing India's nuclear submarine program. He also became an active member of various think tanks until he died in 2007 at 80.

Despite the challenges and pressures these five admirals faced, they managed to retire at the age of 80 or more, a testament to their fitness, dedication, and commitment to their profession and valuable contribution of service to their country.

Indeed, to those who believe that no one in their 60s or beyond has any business being in military service, there are numerous examples of individuals who served their countries' military organizations well past the age of 70. For example, Sir Arthur Harris, also known as "Bomber"

Harris, was Commander-in-Chief of the RAF Bomber Command during World War II. He retired from active service at 65 but was recalled to active duty during the Suez Crisis in 1956 when he was 74. Likewise, Georgy Zhukov, a prominent military leader during World War II, served in the Soviet Red Army until the age of 72. After the war, he held several high-ranking positions, such as Minister of Defense and Chief of the General Staff.

The story of Grace Hopper, portrayed by author James Fell in his book *On This Day in History* ... (2020), illustrates one of the most fascinating stories of the upper limits of age and the military. She was known as the oldest active duty commissioned officer in the Navy of any gender. She was awarded a PhD in mathematics from Yale in 1934. She failed in her attempt to enlist in the Navy during World War II because, at 34, she was too old. Thus, she joined the Naval Reserves and in 1944 was assigned to Harvard's Computation Project. Her work with programming languages led to the creation of one of the earliest commercial computers, which eventually transformed the DOD computer systems from centralized to distributed networks. Military regulations eventually caught up with her, forcing retirement at age 60. However, the following year she was beckoned back with an indefinite assignment, retiring again, then at age 65. But within a year, she was asked to return to active duty with a promotion to captain. She remained in the Navy until her final discharge in 1986, with the rank of commodore.

Understaffed and Overchallenged

There are many reasons why recruiting has hit an impasse. First, because of changing demographics, there is a shrinking population of young people eligible to serve. The prime military recruitment age range (17–24 years old) is now dwarfed by an aging population of Baby Boomers. Second, many potential recruits do not meet the service's physical fitness and health standards. Third, many potential recruits are disqualified due to criminal records, drug use, or moral/ethical issues that conflict with the military's standards of conduct. In addition, the military competes with private companies for skilled and educated individuals. Finally, the private sector offers higher salaries, flexible working hours, and other benefits that make military service less attractive by comparison.

In what we call "conventional warfare," in which soldiers are on a battlefield fighting face-to-face with an enemy combatant, there is no doubt that all commanding officers would want a fit corps of 18-to-21-year-olds. And why is that? In the words of Admiral Dennis McCoy, those are the individuals who are too young to understand the enormous dangers they face. That fearlessness generates physical and psychic energy that makes them formidable opponents. Moreover, because they are too young to understand the hazards and cannot assess the risks associated with their actions, they will gladly rush headlong into situations that more seasoned soldiers would hesitate to try. For this very reason, wars have always been fought by young people, primarily young men.

During the past few decades, technological advancements have introduced different types of warfare, such as that fought by drones and unmanned vehicles. Undoubtedly, many military organizations worldwide believe that investing in technology is the only way to prepare for the next conflict. However, the recent war in Ukraine shows us that conventional warfare will likely persist. Technology will play an increasingly important role in any conflict, but the human element is unlikely ever to disappear.

While researching this book, I've spoken with scores of military veterans from many wars, including World War II, Korea, Vietnam, Iraq, and Afghanistan. To a person, they all agree with one thing. No one wants to raise the lower limit on recruiting new personnel from 18 to 21 or even higher. The reason in all cases is the same. Eighteen-year-olds are uniquely cognitively underdeveloped, allowing them to do jobs that older individuals would think twice about. Sadly, they all believe that the necessity of having fearless warriors outweighs the ethics of sending 18-year-olds into battle.

But what if it's simply impossible to recruit enough 18-to-21-year-olds? Consider that the U.S. military is fighting an uphill battle to encourage enough people to enlist. Indeed, even monetary incentives (signing bonuses of up to $45,000) have proven insufficient. If cash bonuses aren't getting it done, then what? Maybe it's time to reconsider the processes of recruitment and enlistment.

In recent decades several countries have been successful at recruiting people to join their military forces. However, the methods and reasons behind their success vary depending on cultural, social, and economic factors. These countries include Israel, Singapore, Norway, Finland, and South Korea.

Israel has a policy of mandatory military service for both men and women, which has resulted in a high level of participation in the Israel Defense Forces (IDF). Additionally, the nation's strong sense of national identity and the perceived existential threats it faces contribute to a culture that values military service.

Like Israel, Singapore has a policy of mandatory military service for males, known as National Service. The nation's small population and the perceived need to maintain a strong defense force to ensure its sovereignty contribute to a high commitment to military service.

Norway practices conscription for both men and women, and the country has a strong tradition of military service. The Norwegian Armed Forces enjoy a positive public image, and the country's high standard of living and quality of life may contribute to the success of its military recruitment efforts.

Finland also has a conscription system for males and voluntary service for females, and the Finnish Defense Forces are generally viewed positively by the population. In addition, the strong sense of national identity and the historical context of defending the nation's independence contribute to the success of military recruitment in Finland.

South Korea also has mandatory military service for males due to the ongoing tensions with North Korea.

In each case, factors such as mandatory military service, strong national identity, and perceived security threats contribute to successful military recruitment efforts. However, it is essential to note that the success of these recruitment efforts depends on each country's specific social, cultural, and economic contexts.

Would mandatory service work in the United States? Realistically, at this point, it seems unlikely. The United States is not currently at war, there is no perceived immediate threat, and the U.S. military is not hugely popular. However, there may be ways to change that image, perhaps, as a first step, by allowing anyone of any age to enlist or at least to be of service for a year in some capacity. Some alternatives to military service could be civilian service, environmental service, public health service, infrastructure service (e.g., WPA during the Depression), education service, or even disaster relief service. Of course, not everyone is cut out to be a service member, but almost everyone can give back to their nation in one form of service or another.

For youth unprepared for military service, are there better options to assist their transition to responsible adulthood? I believe so. The following are several ideas worth considering:

- National Youth Service Corps—Create government-sponsored programs focused on public service projects, such as disaster relief, infrastructure repair, tutoring students, and assisting the elderly. Such a corps could provide structure, skill-building, and civic engagement.
- Expanded AmeriCorps and Peace Corps—Increase domestic and global service opportunities for 18–25-year-olds. This helps to builds leadership skills, cultural awareness, and a sense of purpose.
- Public Health Service—Non-combat roles improving communities, which may include conducting health education, data analysis, or environmental conservation. Offers valuable experience in uniformed service.
- Skills Training—Paid apprenticeships and vocational programs to gain expertise for in-demand careers. Such training would provide hands-on learning and job prospects after completion.
- Mentorships—Pair young adults with professionals or tradespeople to teach practical skills and offer guidance. Fosters maturity and responsibility.
- Outward Bound—Outdoor challenge programs focused on character development and teamwork; helps develop grit, resilience, and self-confidence.
- Gap Years—Time off between high school and college for structured travel, language study, service projects, or internships. Opportunity for personal growth.

Of course, these initiatives would require funding and infrastructure development. But the benefits would be immense—for both the young participants and society overall. With a coordinated national effort, we can set millions of teenagers on a constructive path to adulthood outside the military, then recruit those truly ready to serve their nation in uniform.

The dilemma of the recruitment shortfall is an issue to which many military leaders are struggling to find a solution. Some policymakers are calling for an expansion of the age limit. Allowing older veterans beyond age 39 to serve in the military is complex and multifaceted, a risk I believe is worth taking. This restriction denies the military an urgent resource at a time when the U.S. needs renewal and strength. The more mature and experienced may lead the way and galvanize enthusiasm and commitment for those who are undecided.

The military serves as a critical pillar of national security, with its effectiveness hinging upon the successful recruitment and retention of highly qualified personnel. Regrettably, existing recruitment strategies have not produced the desired outcomes. Therefore, policymakers and military leaders must prioritize the engagement of seasoned veterans whose maturity and experience can help address the current challenges.

Furthermore, all military institutions must maintain exemplary leadership while concentrating on authentic priorities. Fostering a culture of sustained excellence will attract potential recruits and bolster military morale. In doing so, such leadership and excellence will cultivate a robust sense of resiliency, courage, and esprit de corps that is indispensable to a thriving military force.

Leveraging Older Talent—Lessons from Academia, Law, Medicine, and Politics

Academia relies heavily on older, experienced professors to lead research, teach specialized courses, and mentor students. Mandatory retirement ages have been eliminated, and faculties commonly include actively publishing professors in their 70s and 80s who possess decades of expertise. Their scholarly output and grant funding are invaluable.

Likewise, large law firms actively recruit later-career partners. Their extensive legal experience enables them to manage large, complex cases and provide wise counsel on high-stakes litigation. Clients depend on their seasoned judgment. Many argue cases into their 70s or serve as judges at advanced ages. Their wisdom is a competitive advantage.

Medicine also leans on older clinicians. Hospital chiefs of staff are often in their 60s. Surgeons remain prized into their 70s for specialized technical skills developed over long careers. Geriatricians don't even enter the field until their 40s after decades of prior experience. Patients benefit from providers with extensive knowledge.

In government, legislators and officials with lengthy resumes wield influence. Think of congressional leaders like Strom Thurmond serving into his 100s. Committee chairs and ranking members tend to be senior politicians. Their depth of knowledge on complex policies is unmatched. Executive branch officials and advisors also derive authority from prior roles across the government. Their institutional memory is invaluable. The Senate has also considered minimum age limits: Author Victor Hanson states in his latest book, *The Dying Citizen*, senators must be 30 years old, not 25—on the idea that adults are soberer and more experienced (if less idealistic and impulsive) at 30 (Hanson, 2021).

The military has analogous specialized roles—technical, strategic, and teaching—where lengthy experience fosters unique expertise. Like academia retaining eminent scholars, the armed forces should retain seasoned analysts, instructors, advisors, and leaders. Their mastery and wisdom, honed over decades, can help to solve problems and guide strategy in ways younger service members cannot.

Changing Military Culture to Value Mastery Over Youth

To shift traditional military cultural bias toward youth, concrete steps must come from the top down. Performance systems should incorporate new metrics such as longevity, expertise, and institutional knowledge that increase with age. Awards and decorations can recognize continuity of service and excellence in mentorship—achievements enabled by longer careers.

Promotion timelines could gradually increase with additional meritocratic gates at key general and flag officer ranks tied to experience, not age. Unit command qualification assessments could weigh candidates' specialized skills more and physical benchmarks less, beyond initial career stages.

Leadership messaging should explicitly value deep expertise. Narratives praising older members' contributions must counter outdated assumptions of decline. And career flexibility through veteran reserve components would enable seasoned personnel to phase to training and advisory roles rather than face binary stay-or-retire decisions.

With buy-in across ranks, the armed forces can elevate mastery over youth, embrace its seasoned veterans, and recognize their wealth of knowledge. Their mentorship and perspective honed over decades of service strengthens the force's skill and character. You don't learn warfare from books—you learn it from old soldiers.

On Capitol Hill, congressional veterans constitute a dwindling but influential cohort informing defense policy and oversight. They lend firsthand experience to complex military matters. And leaders like John McCain used their deep knowledge to champion reform. Their longtime service on armed services committees provides institutional memory to complement term-limited legislators.

Within the executive branch, older officials applying decades of uniformed experience to policy roles are invaluable. Former Marine Corps General Jim Mattis led the DOD in his 60s, bringing his 44 years in uniform to manage strategy, budgets, and procurement. At the State Department, long-serving diplomats lend perspective to security partnerships nurtured over successive administrations. And at higher levels, their advice on military options and risks carries weight that novice civilian appointees may lack.

Yet rigid military career timelines force many leaders into premature retirement, stripping this expertise just when political leadership needs it most. Enabling flexible uniformed or civil service would retain more elder voices to strengthen oversight. Their operational mastery and objectivity are assets no textbook or junior officer can replace. Their wisdom must be leveraged far longer.

Potential Cost Savings from Older Recruits

Older service members and veterans entering recruiting pools can yield notable cost efficiencies:

Education/GI Bill—Older individuals will likely have completed education and training, avoiding tuition and GI Bill expenditure. Recouping prior investments versus paying for recruits' multi-year education saves millions.

Family housing allowances—Providing costly on-base family housing is unnecessary for older adults whose children have left home. Savings can be redirected.

Moving costs—Since older recruits are less likely to relocate families due to children or spouses' careers, permanent change of station expenditures are reduced.

Initial training outlays—For veterans who have already completed initial entry and specialty training, avoiding repeat investments saves billions. Retaining their readiness is vastly cheaper than developing it anew.

Leadership and Experience

A common perception in many societies is that with age comes diminishing strength, vitality, and usefulness. Older people are seen as a burden, occupying space and consuming resources without making meaningful contributions. This notion manifests in the rigid age restrictions upheld by most militaries worldwide, which favor the purported vigor of youth over the wisdom of experience.

However, modern research increasingly reveals the flaws in such ageist assumptions. In recent generations, medical science has increased typical life expectancy by over a decade. Today's healthy 65-year-old can contribute far more over additional lifetime years than in decades past. Research (Bersin and Chamorro-Premuzic, 2019; Faremeh et al., 2019) shows physical and mental fitness vary tremendously based on individuals' lifestyle factors, regardless of age. Evaluating ability rather than assuming age-based limitations is crucial. Technological advances accommodate certain physical deficits, enabling those with only partial impairments to serve effectively. Assistance can optimize individuals' existing capabilities.

Cognitive skills like critical thinking, judgment, and problem-solving reliably improve with age and peak late in careers. Mastery comes through years of practice honing expertise. Studies (Warburton et al., 2006) indicate that regular exercise and healthy habits can help maintain physical and psychological functioning well into old age. The seasoned minds of healthy older adults exhibit strengths such as structured problem-solving, emotional stability, nuanced judgment, and seeing complex issues from multiple perspectives. Data from a study in Canada (Rivers and Barnett, 2016) revealed workers aged 65–80 performed more stable work, with less variability and with a more consistent cognitive performance compared to their counterparts, young adults aged 20–31. With careful assessments and modern assistive tools, many still-capable older recruits can clearly contribute to mission-critical billets. Outdated biases overlook a wealth of experience at society's disposal. Such abilities are invaluable on the battlefield and in command positions.

General George C. Marshall, the architect of victory in World War II, was advanced in years when he took the helm. Marshall's composed leadership, strategic vision, and ability to manage clashing egos were instrumental to the Allied victory. Winston Churchill was 65 when he became Britain's wartime Prime Minister, inspiring the nation through years of peril with his masterful oratory skills nurtured over decades. Their momentous achievements disprove the notion that vital leadership is the sole domain of the young.

Likewise, frontline duties need not be restricted by age, with proper conditioning and selective placement matching abilities.

As warfare evolves into new technological and informational realms, traits correlated with maturity—such as judicious discernment, nuanced understanding of geopolitics, and coolness under fire—may prove more decisive than sheer physical prowess. The most effective forces will blend wisdom and strength from both ends of the age spectrum.

Just as demographic changes are forcing retirement ages upward in the civilian world, similar shifts in orientation may serve the military well. An evolving force harnessing competencies from young and old could open new pathways for qualified individuals to contribute substantial decades of their lives in service of the nation.

With open minds and measured analysis, policies can balance harnessing youthful vigor and mature expertise. But change requires relinquishing the comfort of long-held assumptions. Those of advanced years who retain the skills and will to serve honorably must not be barred or sidelined solely according to an arbitrary number. Their knowledge and talents can empower a stronger, wiser military if given the opportunity.

CHAPTER 8

Resilience Screening and Training

The childhood shows the man as morning shows the day.

—MILTON, *PARADISE LOST*

During my first mobilization under Operation *Noble Eagle*, a young recruit named JJ, barely 20 with a TIS of one year, was sent to a field hospital for a fitness for duty (theater) evaluation. He exhibited tremors and profound shaking from head to toe, and his speech was halting and quivering. He was soon to be flown out to Iraq. Although he had enlisted in the U.S. Army, then aged 19, and sworn to defend his country, he was weakened by debilitating anxiety and destined to be a casualty in a harsh and unforgiving terrain with little or no mental health services available, an easy decision, "not to deploy."

Another recruit, TJ, was admitted for suicidal behavior and for driving his car erratically in traffic. He returned from deployment five weeks previously, anxious and depressed, admitting, "I can't eat or sleep since I returned." He complained of "God-awful treatment in the military" and said he was treated in a degrading matter. His checkered history was punctuated with chronic depression since age nine and episodic suicidal ideation since age 12, with a suicide attempt by hanging at age 17. His recent episode involved cutting his wrists, saying, "It felt good to feel pain."

TJ's troubled childhood was marked by abuse, with a long history of psychological issues and no treatment. His coping behaviors included self-harm, e.g., head-bashing and cutting. His mood brightened after being told he would be discharged under chapter 5–13, personality disorder.

Another service member, DJ, a 29-year-old with one tour of 12 months in Iraq and looking at another deployment to theater, appeared for his evaluation missing the strings attached to his combat boots and wearing no belt. He had just informed his sergeant that he was thinking of hanging himself. His precipitating event was being charged with a DUI the previous week. He had been drinking a fifth a day since his return from Iraq and had reported suicidal thoughts but affirmed that he would never act upon them, stating, "I would go to hell for doing it."

DJ had no psychiatric history of mental health issues before military service or suicide attempts. However, he was unhappy with his command. His punishment for the DUI meant a loss of rank and 45 days of extra duty with a denial of 45 days of leave in the future. In addition, he protested that he would not be able to say goodbye to his parents in the Midwest before he left for Iraq. From all appearances, he was a perfect athletic specimen with great height, bone structure, and a look of lean and mean bulk muscle to spare, an ideal fighting machine. Before leaving the interview, he stated, "I saw some of my soldiers eat their last meal."

Everyone has a potential breaking point when the trauma threshold has been breached. However, resilient individuals arguably have substantially greater predictability of mental health survival under stress. Some people cope well with adversity, even being strengthened by the experience, while others may develop severe and persistent psychopathology after such exposure (Rutter, 2000; Bonanno, 2004).

According to Kim Waldron (2008), more than 43,000 U.S. troops listed as medically unfit for combat in the weeks before their scheduled deployment to Iraq or Afghanistan since 2003 were sent anyway. Furthermore, statistics show that the number of troops found non-deployable but still sent to combat fluctuated from 10,854 in 2003 to 5,397 in 2005 and back up to 9,140 in 2007. Unit commanders decide whether a service member gets sent into battle, although doctors can recommend against deployment due to a medical issue.

A strong argument can be made that young recruits should be given a thorough screening before sending them into combat. Reactivity to a negative situation or unfulfilled expectation can diminish a soldier's ability to problem-solve or make wise decisions. Wrongful decision-making and maladaptive coping are the enemies of survival; for too many, it can trigger an impulse to escape. Desperation may overtake them, and they end their life. Stressful personal events can be a precursor for the cascade of vulnerability. They can lead to a dark hole with no way out, a sense of profound inner emptiness, and a retreat to their cerebral foxholes.

The difference between those who survive and thrive in the military and those who do not, like TJ and DJ, often comes down to resilience. Resilience attributes include social support, self-esteem, optimism, coping skills, and factors such as genetics and childhood experiences, such as abuse and neglect, which can have a lasting impact. Individuals with strong social networks are more likely to be resilient in the face of stressors. DJ was considered a loner; thus, not seeing his parents before leaving for his second deployment was crucial, given that his social support network was very thin.

Army psychiatrist Dr. Richard Schneider draws upon his active-duty experience and shares his thoughts about young active-duty service members and resilience:

> We now understand that adolescence, the final period of brain development, extends beyond the teenage years into the early twenties. The implication of this was that although many of the young soldiers in the sixties and early seventies may have been old enough to serve, they were not necessarily ready to cope with the demands that the military placed on them, especially in a hostile jungle setting. Their attributes of maturity and resiliency were often still evolving and stabilizing, and would sometimes be inadequate for the challenges they encountered. Another concern was that during the Vietnam war troops were sent over individually, which negatively impacted morale. The military learned through this failure, however, and subsequently began training and deploying units together, which greatly improved camaraderie and morale. The resulting social support and group cohesion turned out to be crucial for helping these young people to adapt to the struggles and challenges for military service. Their being part of a team added a new incentive or acquiring and displaying resilience and fortitude.

A study on 10 Vietnam War veterans who did not develop post-traumatic stress disorder, despite being exposed to intense combat, revealed a recurring set of coping techniques. These remarkable individuals demonstrated an active approach to tackling their challenges, including strong social skills and a clear sense of control over their lives.

They consciously prioritized their calmness, judgment, and connections with others while adhering to their moral principles and finding meaning amidst the chaos. Instead of viewing the war as an opportunity to prove their masculinity or surrendering to feelings of helplessness, they approached it as a dangerous situation to be managed effectively, with the goal of survival. Additionally, they refrained from succumbing to rage (Herman, 1992).

Numerous studies have shown that resilient individuals significantly differ in their cognitive and behavioral responses to stressors. For example, in a study by Fredrickson et al. (2003), participants exposed to an adverse event (watching a film depicting injuries and death) showed increased negative emotions, physiological arousal, and immune system functioning. However, those participants with high levels of resilience showed faster recovery rates in both physiological (blood pressure, heart rate, decline of stress hormones) and psychological (anxiety) variables.

Steinberg and Ritzmann (1990) use the term "resistance" to depict homeostasis or steadfastness in coping with adversity, and use resilience as a healthy adaptive process to restore steadfastness or homeostasis from a state of disturbance. Positive emotions, such as laughter and humor, are perceived as reducers of distress following aversive events by undoing or neutralizing negative emotions (Bonanno, 2004; Fredrickson et al., 1998).

The implications of these findings are significant, particularly in the arena of stress management training. Resilience can be improved through various training interventions, such as cognitive behavioral therapies, mindfulness interventions, or resilience training programs. By improving resilience, service members may be better equipped to cope with the demands of military service, reduce stress, improve overall well-being, and rehabilitate those who are struggling to adapt and succeed in their line of duty.

Too much attention on age in the recruitment and enlistment process can distract from attention to the emotional health of many young recruits. Tragically, all service branches fail to consider histories of psychological malnourishment and physical and emotional abuse. As I've encountered numerous washouts and dishonorable discharges, there is often a pattern of struggles and failures to adapt to the stressors and challenges of military life as soldiers.

Rethinking Screening

Age as a metric is an easy way to screen. Still, it fails to account for traits such as resilience and adaptability that, regardless of biological age, might predict future success more accurately. Certainly, screening out candidates based on severe emotional and psychological baggage would seem like an easy and obvious mandate. Yet, the U.S. military has never seen fit to do so.

There are many requisites for healthy human development and emotional maturity. Harry Stack Sullivan, the father of interpersonal psychiatry, stated his theory of personality as a phenomenon shaped by relationships shared with other people (Sullivan, 1953). Maybe there is a second chance for redirection and healing of those young recruits who never received nurturance in childhood. Having a strong mentor (such as a sergeant or NCO) could be a turning point for them in their development, leading to increased emotional maturity and resilience.

The determinants of human behavior are multidimensional (cultural, spiritual, biological, social, and psychological). Fundamentally, the primary requisite for success in the military and life is healthy self-esteem, a major factor missing in the aforementioned illustrated cases. There is no specific age for this attribute, albeit it is the ingredient that propels in motion the inner core of one's sense of self-respect and personal worth, the pathway to confidence and self-reliance. To get there, you can't take the elevator; you must take the stairs. Those in their late teens or early 20s who join the military have youth on their side, a chance to grow and learn from their mistakes, but only if they survive. Resilience screening is to assess candidates' past experiences and coping strategies. For example, an applicant who has overcome significant adversity in life—such as a history of childhood abuse or combat exposure—might be viewed as more resilient than someone without similar experiences. Likewise, individuals who demonstrate proactive coping skills—such as seeking social support, engaging in problem-solving, or practicing mindfulness—might be flagged as potential high-resilience candidates.

Another approach to resilience screening is to use standardized psychological assessments. Several validated resilience measures exist, such as the Resilience Scale (Wagnild and Young, 1993) and Brief Resilience Scale (Smith et al., 2008).

Resilience training has been shown to be an effective preventative measure against post-traumatic stress disorder. A recent study (Doody et al., 2021) conducted in the military found it to be measurably protective to help prevent PTSD among soldiers. Success was noted with the use of pre-deployment which utilized mindfulness and behavioral techniques.

The training was particularly effective in reducing symptoms of PTSD related to hyperarousal, avoidance, and intrusion. These findings suggest that resilience training can be valuable in preventing PTSD among military personnel.

The great Chinese philosopher Lao Tzu wrote about resilience 2,600 years ago in the *Tao Te Ching*, concluding that resiliency is an essential quality in all long-term success:

> A man is born gentle and weak.
> At his death he is hard and stiff.
> Green plants are tender and filled with sap.
> At their death they are withered and dry.
>
> Therefore the stiff and unbending is the disciple of death.
> The gentle and yielding is the disciple of life.
>
> Thus an army without flexibility never wins a battle.
> A tree that is unbending is easily broken.
>
> The hard and soft will fall.
> The soft and weak will overcome.

Ideally, we want U.S. military recruits who are able, willing, and psychologically strong enough to cope with fighting battles. But watching their comrades die and suffer unimaginable trauma in service is, for many, unbearable. Soldiers' last words, whether spoken or written, can sometimes be the most poignant and revealing, illustrating the raw truth of service members' sacrifice to the nation. Young combat veterans' last words and thoughts in the Iraq War were punctuated: "stressed, scared, paranoid or fearful, death everywhere, it waits for me." During the Iraq War, the average age of the infantry was 19, and the average rank of soldiers killed was private first class (Stanton, 2004).

For men and women who, for whatever reason, come into the service with baggage (self-defeating and maladaptive coping mechanisms), the consequence is that they are burdened at entry with formidable challenges and the prospects of marginal success. Changing entrenched emotional patterns of reactivity can be difficult, if not impossible. However, some can at least have a fighting chance with a rehabilitative skill approach.

Like many institutions, the military has a limited capacity to identify people with psychological difficulties. The military does not have or use any special test to measure mood or emotional disturbances. If that weren't bad enough, almost no military organizations, with the possible exception of Israel, let psychologists interview inductees before they join. Military service is difficult enough for the young and immature. Still, it can end badly for those burdened with insurmountable psychological obstacles stemming from an abusive, depraved family background.

There are now tests available for hiring police and safety officers which predict how the officer will fare in the first year of service. They are used on workers to detect their capacity for suitability. But there is nothing like this test in U.S. military screening. However, the tools to screen and determine cognitive capacity or aptitude are readily available.

Irrespective of age, one measure that does predict success in military service is resilience. Learning about young men and women's trauma history, of what they have endured before military service, can reveal salient factors about their adaptability and coping. These are metrics that are elusive to standardized tests or psychometrics. An article published in *Psychology Today*, "The Best Predictor of Future Behavior Is ... Past Behavior," the maxim is not seen as entirely useless, but it ignores base rates and the age-crime curve" (Franklin, 2013).

I would argue that resilience skill training should be a priority of the military. If such orientation is given early enough, it could shift the scale from unfit to fit for many enlistees who find themselves in a sea of doubt and uncertainty about whether they will succeed in the challenges of military service.

In his book *The Undoing Project*, Michael Lewis shares how famed psychologists Daniel Kahneman and Amos Tversky devised an approach for the Israeli military to select fit candidates. Young men who applied for army officer training were considered good prospects not just of who could take charge but how much they could cooperate in contributing to the group effort (Lewis, 2017).

Kahneman and Tversky implemented a screening program that took a holistic approach to evaluating candidates across multiple dimensions, such as motivation, skill sets, and psychological factors, to assess their potential fit and contribution to the military. This approach was more comprehensive than just measuring intellectual or physical abilities alone.

One of their most important innovations was developing the "combat readiness" score that weighted interpersonal, motivational, and emotional factors more heavily than IQ or physical traits. Through their research, Kahneman and Tversky identified qualities such as authority acceptance, a sense of responsibility, and empathy as critical to success, potentially even more so than sheer brainpower or strength.

To surface these psychological traits, they found that peer ratings and semi-structured interviews were effective evaluation methods, complementing cognitive or physical testing. Peer opinions helped identify both positive and negative leadership potential in candidates. Their screening tools also helped uncover mental health issues, over-confidence, impulsivity, and other "red flags" that could compromise performance and endanger others. These psychological factors proved very predictive of successful service.

Rather than a one-size-fits-all approach, Kahneman and Tversky also tailored selection criteria and tests to the needs of different units, developing specialized screening for roles like pilots versus infantry. They implemented continuous assessment after the initial screening to further evaluate military performance and potential, rather than just making a one-time static selection decision.

Personality testing worked in this case because it looked for loose correlations between traits and behavior. Loose correlations of two things are related, but not always in the same way. Height and weight might be related, for example, but there are variations, with people tending to be heavier at the bottom of their height range and lighter at the top.

Before the era of personality testing, American psychologist Edward Thorndike, in his research of the selection process of recruits during World War I, found when army officers were asked to rate their men according to prowess and then assess them for leadership, the first rating seeped into the second. Thus, the rating officer, who was impressed by their physique, also believed that the recruit was superior in other ways. This perception became known as the "halo effect" (Thorndike, 1920).

Personality testing, especially with validity scales, can provide factual information to assist in making reliable assumptions in the selection process for military recruiting, yet few military organizations use them. Why is that? It probably stems from the fact that recruiting people into the military is often difficult because the objective is not to screen people out but to get the largest possible base of candidates. The winnowing process happens after they join, usually by self-selection, which is somehow seen as a better system, even though the cost in terms of lives, training, and equipment is orders of magnitude greater than the cost of a psychological test.

If we must send these young recruits off to war, I believe their best chance of survival is tantamount to their capability to withstand shock and adversity without rupturing their psyche. Resilience training for many is of paramount importance regardless of whether they are 18, 25, 35, or have no underlying psychopathology.

Training Military Troops in the Development of Resilience

Resilience has been a measure of strength throughout the history of military duty but perhaps never so strenuously tested as for those who served as POWs. The story of Louis Zamperini is one of triumph in the face of adversity. As a young Air Corpsman, Zamperini was a crew member of a B-24 bomber that was shot down during a mission over the Pacific in 1943. For 48 days, he and two other crew members drifted on a life raft, surviving on meager rations, braving shark attacks, dehydration, and being exposed to the elements, only to be captured by Japanese soldiers on a lonely island, which at first blush they thought was their sanctuary. Zamperini was taken to a series of POW camps before ending up in his final torture dungeon, where he endured three years of hell. His life became a desperate struggle for survival between his captor-torturer and his will to live. His ultimate challenge, however, came after his release. After his survival and return home, his next stressful challenge was the post-traumatic revisitation of his painful memories of his POW trauma. He was plagued by a demonic-like haunting of his past and a desperation to hunt down and kill his hated captor, an obsession that would consume him until resolution years later.

Resilience refers to the ability to adapt and cope with adversity, whether it be a traumatic event, chronic stress, or daily challenges. This ability involves many cognitive, emotional, behavioral, and in Zamperini's case, spiritual factors that help individuals maintain a sense of hope, optimism, and mastery in the face of adversity. One of the key features of resilience is the ability to bounce back from setbacks and persevere in pursuing goals.

The Comprehensive Soldier and Family Fitness (CSF2) program launched in 2011 provides a holistic approach to building resilience, including physical, emotional, social, spiritual, and family training. Another program, the Resilience, Risk Reduction and Suicide Prevention (R3SP) initiative, aims to reduce suicides and enhance the resilience of soldiers, focusing on risk identification, prevention, and treatment strategies.

Military operations present unique challenges to military personnel, such as exposure to dangerous and stressful situations, separation from family, and long working hours, which can lead to various psychological and physical challenges. Often, this requires coping with adversity, persisting in the face of challenges, and bouncing back from setbacks.

Among the latest programs and interventions is Comprehensive Airman Fitness (CAF), a holistic approach that focuses on the overall well-being of military personnel. "The program was launched in 2014, a cultural shift in how to maintain fitness and to hold each other accountable by learning the fundamentals of four pillars (mental, physical, social, and spiritual—a strengthening of beliefs, values which sustain a sense of wellbeing/purpose. It was a spiritual conversion in 1949 for Zamperini when he attended a Billy Graham service in Los Angeles. From that time forward, he experienced freedom from his obsession with vengeance toward his perpetrator of torture. Subsequently, he became a motivational speaker for resiliency, faith, and forgiveness.

In addition to the existing resilience programs, the military could benefit from incorporating innovative strategies that promote mental well-being, enhance coping skills, and foster a supportive environment for service members.

Nature-based therapy can have a profound impact on mental health and well-being. Integrating nature-based therapies, such as wilderness retreats and adventure therapy, into resilience training can help service members reconnect with the natural world, reduce stress, and develop problem-solving skills. These activities can include team-building exercises, outdoor survival skills training, and mindfulness practices in nature.

Virtual reality exposure therapy (VRET) uses cutting-edge technology to help soldiers gradually confront and manage traumatic experiences or phobias in a controlled and safe environment. By simulating various stress-inducing situations, VRET would allow service members to develop coping strategies and build resilience to real-life challenges.

Mentorship programs would pair experienced service members with newer recruits can help build resilience by fostering supportive relationships, sharing coping strategies, and providing guidance during challenging times. This intergenerational exchange of knowledge and experience can enhance personal growth and boost morale.

Even canine therapy, in which service members are paired with specially trained therapy dogs, can provide comfort, reduce stress, and improve emotional well-being. Canine therapy could facilitate social interaction and promote a sense of belonging among military personnel.

Equine therapy has also been effective for treating PTSD. Veterans with post-traumatic stress symptoms are often distrustful of others and anxious. In this therapeutic milieu, they learn how to build trust by becoming aware of their subtle nuances which transfer to the horse. In the process of learning to reassure the animal that they have trust and confidence, emotional healing occurs combined with behavioral changes, e.g., diminished anxiety.

How Understanding the Brain Can Boost Military Resilience

Advances in neuroscience research have shed light on the neural mechanisms underlying resilience, with important implications for strengthening military training programs. By understanding the brain systems involved in resilience and implementing insights from neuroscience, the military can develop optimized training approaches that build this vital skill.

Fundamentally, resilience arises from neural circuits enabling emotional regulation, stress management, cognitive flexibility, and the formation of social bonds. Neuroimaging studies have identified key brain regions and networks tied to these capabilities. Specific brain areas and circuits enable resilience abilities, such as regulating emotions, managing stress, focusing mentally, and bonding socially. For instance, resilience is associated with greater volume and activity in the ventromedial prefrontal cortex (mid portion) which binds together large-scale networks, supports emotional regulation, and controls fear and anxiety. In other words, it puts the brakes on overreacting to stress. These networks dampen amygdala reactivity to modulate anxiety and fear responses. Resilient individuals also demonstrate reduced responses, e.g., social exclusion, enabling maintained social engagement during stress.

Understanding these neural foundations suggests new training approaches. Directly exercising "resilience muscles" in the brain strengthens them. Mindfulness builds up prefrontal circuits for emotion control. Gradually facing manageable stress can tune the brain's stress response system. Virtual reality simulating challenges let us practice neural resilience skills.

Measuring brain activity provides concrete feedback on whether training is working. Seeing increases in prefrontal activity shows better regulation. Tracking chemical messengers like norepinephrine gives a biomarker for stress resilience gains. Technologies like brain stimulation can also enhance training. Non-invasive stimulation of key resilience nodes and cognitive or emotional challenges have shown promise for improving resilience skills. And highly immersive VR scenarios activating neural stress resilience systems provide vivid, experiential training with neuroscience-based design principles.

The prefrontal cortex comes to the fore when we consider the importance of prefrontal activity and its important function of modulating and regulating stimuli. It is all the more reason to rethink the arbitrary rule of sending teenagers into the fray of combat. When confronted with some of the most fearful stressors of military service, the carnage and torture of battle, a mature brain would, at minimum, give the service member a better chance for survival. Being a battle-tested service member does not guarantee resilience. Based on my professional experience with military combatants and affirmed by numerous psychiatrists, there is an inverse relationship (based on the severity of combat experience) between increased resilience and length of combat.

Of course, character, social support, and other factors are still vital for resilience. We shouldn't focus just on the brain in isolation. But adding neuroscience-based techniques to military training is powerful. It targets the source—our brain's resilience machinery. Fine-tuning the brain to be stress-fit and emotionally tough gives service members an extra advantage in managing adversity. So, applying emerging neuroscience can transform military resilience preparation to help today's troops thrive in turbulent times.

The brain is a big player in resilience, and understanding its inner workings enables more direct training. Exercising neural pathways, tracking brain changes, and using brain-focused technologies can optimize military programs for performing under pressure. Resilience lives in our character and our central command, namely our brain.

Can Resilience Be Trained?

Factors that influence the success of resiliency training include the individual's motivation to participate in the program, the quality of the program delivery, and the severity of the stressor. For example, individuals who are highly motivated to participate in the training are more likely to experience positive outcomes. Additionally, the quality of the training delivery, including the facilitator's skill, the training program's format, and the duration, also plays a significant role in the success of resiliency training.

The benefits of resiliency training have shown that improvements may last up to one year. In addition, studies have shown that this training can improve an individual's ability to cope with stress and adversity, reduce symptoms of depression and anxiety, and improve overall well-being. However, resiliency training as a technique to permanently change an individual's personality has yet to be discovered.

Military Resilience Around the World

The United States is not alone in trying to address and improve resilience among its ranks. Other countries, including Australia, Canada, the United Kingdom, Israel, the Netherlands, New Zealand, Sweden, Finland, Norway, and South Korea, all have similar programs, some of which have proven successful.

Australian Defense Force (ADF), for example, has implemented a program called "Battle SMART" (Self-Management and Resilience Training), designed to teach military personnel cognitive and behavioral skills to manage stress, build resilience, and maintain peak performance. The program includes self-awareness, goal setting, problem-solving, and cognitive restructuring.

Canadian Armed Forces (CAF) introduced the "Road to Mental Readiness" (R2MR) program, which aims to improve mental health, enhance resilience, and reduce the stigma associated with seeking help for mental health issues. The R2MR program focuses on mental health education, stress management, building social support networks, and fostering a culture of understanding and acceptance of mental health challenges.

The United Kingdom Ministry of Defense (MoD) developed a resilience training program called "TRM" (Trauma Risk Management). TRM is a peer-led program designed to support personnel exposed to traumatic events, identify those at risk of developing psychological distress, and facilitate timely access to professional help. In addition, the program emphasizes early intervention, normalization of reactions to trauma, and the importance of social support.

Israeli Defense Forces (IDF) implemented a resilience-building program called "Mental Training for Operational Readiness" (METOR), which focuses on enhancing psychological resilience, improving decision-making under pressure, and fostering adaptability. METOR incorporates cognitive behavioral techniques, mindfulness practices, and simulations of stressful scenarios to help soldiers develop effective coping strategies.

New Zealand Defense Force (NZDF) established a "Mental Health and Well-being Strategy," emphasizing the importance of resilience training, early intervention, and mental health education. The strategy includes mental health awareness campaigns, workshops on building resilience, and access to support services.

Royal Netherlands Army introduced the "Mental Fitness Training" program, which focuses on enhancing soldiers' mental resilience, stress management, and overall well-being. The program includes training in coping mechanisms, cognitive behavioral techniques, and team-building exercises.

Swedish Armed Forces have implemented a program called "Psychological Defense," which focuses on mental resilience, stress management, and communication skills. In addition, the program emphasizes the importance of self-awareness, self-regulation, and effective coping strategies in maintaining mental well-being and operational readiness.

Norwegian Armed Forces have established the "Stress Resilience Training" program, which aims to develop soldiers' ability to withstand and recover from stressors encountered during military service. The program includes psychoeducation, relaxation techniques, and exposure to stress-inducing scenarios to develop adaptive coping strategies.

Finnish Defense Forces created the "Comprehensive Soldier Fitness" program, which focuses on the overall well-being of military personnel, including physical, mental, social, and spiritual aspects. The program includes resilience training, mental health education, and support services to help soldiers maintain their well-being during military service.

South Korean Military has implemented a program called "Mental Health and Resilience Training," which aims to enhance soldiers' mental resilience, improve communication skills, and reduce the stigma associated with seeking help for mental health issues. The program includes stress management, problem-solving, and cognitive behavioral techniques.

According to scholarly databases and literature reviews, programs for teaching resilience that have emerged outside the military are seen as the most promising and evidence-based approaches. One which is applicable to young adults is Stress Management and Resiliency Training (SMART), a group-based program that combines cognitive behavioral and mindfulness techniques to decrease stress and enhance resilience in young adults. The program includes eight weekly sessions delivered by trained facilitators and targets seven core modules: awareness, regulating emotions, clarifying values, identifying strengths, building connections, mindfulness, and moving toward resilience goals. The program has been evaluated in several studies and has demonstrated significant improvements in resilience and reducing symptoms of depression, anxiety, and stress in adults.

No single program is the best. Still, from the sheer number of military organizations that attempt to train resilience, it's clear that resilience is well understood to be an essential ingredient in the psychological makeup of troops. It is time that the U.S. military recognizes how resilience training can be a solid investment in the long-term well-being of battle-ready forces and those who serve as support staff.

Psychiatrist and former Army colonel, Richard Schneider, in a recent interview (2023), shared his view of resilience from his active-duty years with enlistees/recruits:

> Resilience was often an attribute of those who wanted to serve, who had volunteered to serve, who were excited to be in the military and proud to be part of a unit. In contrast, there was often a lack of resilience in conscripted people. A sub-attribute of resilience is that balance between self and the unit or cause. More narcissistic individuals may struggle with developing resilience, as setbacks can feel like a blow to their worldview. Those who see themselves as part of a whole and focus on shared goals rather than personal achievements are better able to bounce back and be resilient.

Richard Schneider emphasizes another sub-attribute:

> ... spirituality or sense of something beyond one's life and circumstances. Soldiers with a strong spiritual sense can see the value in putting their lives on the line for their unit, as they believe their souls will live on and that there is more to life than just their breathing and heartbeat. This belief can contribute to their resilience, as they may feel their sacrifice for the cause is worth it and will be rewarded in the future.

An excellent example of this is Sergeant Alvin York, the famous conscientious objector from Tennessee who, during World War I, killed at least 30 enemy soldiers and captured more than 100 others, for which he was awarded the Congressional Medal of Honor. Even though he believed that killing others was wrong and went against his religious beliefs, he decided that American liberty and the safety of the United States was a moral imperative that outweighed religious doctrine. As a result, he went into battle willing to lay down his own life so that the United States might remain safe and free.

CHAPTER 9

A New Strategy for Psychiatry in the Military

During World War II there were many instances of young soldiers who were involved in intense combat scenarios where split-second action made the difference between life and death. The following is a portrayal of an actual example, "Throw the hand grenade," the colonel ordered, but the 18-year-old soldier froze, like a motion picture stuck on one frame, his right hand squeezing the hand grenade with the index finger on the pin. The target was a machine-gun nest of Germans firing at the young soldier's comrades less than 100 yards away. As a result of his inaction, many of his comrades were killed. The young infantry soldier, Ralph, remained paralyzed from that day forward. His life would never be the same; his right index finger was useless.

War happens in seconds, but the memories can haunt soldiers forever. As illustrated in David Morris's book, *The Evil Hours*, psychologists have referred to this phenomenon as fight, flight, or freeze. "War happens in seconds, but it can last a life time, the memories, the trauma. Those who survived and had witnessed such pain and death had the same instinct of those who died but found a way to live." Morris aptly states, "The demonic night and its product, the nightmare, have always been a special hell for survivors."

Based on my clinical experience and review of available literature, young soldiers like Ralph may be at a higher risk of experiencing mental health issues than older soldiers and, as a result, may have an increased need for psychiatric treatment. As mentioned previously, several factors contribute to this heightened risk among young service members.

First, younger individuals are still developing emotionally and psychologically, which can make them more vulnerable to the stresses and traumas associated with military service. Second, soldiers under the age of 21 may have limited experience in coping with adversity and stress, which could make it more challenging for them to navigate the unique demands of military life. Third, executive function may be compromised for those with an underdeveloped prefrontal cortex, which is the case with adolescents. Fourth, younger soldiers are often assigned to combat roles, which can expose them to traumatic events and increase their risk of developing mental health issues such as PTSD, depression, and anxiety.

A Brief History of U.S. Military Psychiatric Treatments

The history of psychiatric treatments in the U.S. military is a tale of perseverance and adaptation in the face of unique mental health challenges military personnel face. From the early days of recognizing the impact of war on soldiers' mental health to the development of innovative approaches, the U.S. military has come a long way in addressing the psychological well-being of its members. The effects of war on soldiers' mental health have been recognized since ancient times. However, it wasn't until the American Civil War that the U.S. military began to pay closer attention to this issue. At that time, soldiers who experienced fatigue, anxiety, and nightmares were diagnosed with "soldier's heart" or nostalgia. While a clinical understanding of these conditions was limited, it marked an essential first step in acknowledging the psychological toll of war.

The concept of shell shock emerged during World War I, when thousands of soldiers experienced symptoms such as tremors, confusion, and memory loss after exposure to heavy artillery fire. This condition was also referred to as "shell shock." As a result, the U.S. military began to develop early forms of psychiatric treatment, such as "forward psychiatry," which aimed to treat soldiers close to the frontlines and return them to duty as soon as possible.

During World War I, triage involved evaluating soldiers' mental health and prioritizing treatment based on the severity of their symptoms.

Forward psychiatry aimed to treat soldiers close to the frontlines, emphasizing the importance of rapid intervention. Techniques used during this time included suggestion therapy, hypnosis, and restorative procedures such as providing food, sleep, and warmth.

World War II saw further advancements in the understanding and treatment of war-related mental health issues. Karl Menninger (known as the Sigmund Freud of America) made monumental contributions to psychiatry as the most prolific writer of his time. His brother, William Menninger, served under the surgeon general during World War II as a brigadier general. He was pivotal in forging psychiatry as an acceptable science and practice in the military. I had the pleasure of having his son as my mentor/supervisor during my residency years at Menningers. The term "combat stress reaction" (CSR) was introduced to describe a range of psychological symptoms experienced by soldiers in combat. In World War II, the military's approach to CSR was more systematic, with the establishment of Combat Exhaustion Treatment Centers, providing soldiers with rest, nourishment, and brief psychotherapy. The aim was to facilitate a rapid return to duty. Treatment approaches included supportive counseling, relaxation techniques, and medications such as sedatives and anti-anxiety drugs.

The Vietnam War brought the concept of PTSD to the forefront of military psychiatry. The psychological impact of the war on returning veterans led to increased awareness of PTSD and its long-term effects. In 1980, PTSD was officially recognized as a psychiatric disorder by the American Psychiatric Association, leading to more research and development of treatments for veterans suffering from this condition. Following the Vietnam War, group therapy became a popular treatment modality for veterans with PTSD. Group therapy allowed veterans to share their experiences and emotions, fostering a sense of camaraderie and understanding. Exposure therapy, which involves gradually exposing patients to the traumatic event in a controlled and safe environment, was also introduced to help veterans confront and process traumatic memories.

Like rap groups (a gathering of people to take part in discussion), group psychotherapy also provides opportunities for social (peer) support and ventilation. But group psychotherapy, as with rap groups, does not usually help to resolve the veteran's problems in his home life; this has been a major weakness. Nevertheless, I concur with other therapists (Frick and Bogart, 1981) that psychoanalytically oriented therapy with groups and families can effectively alter behavioral patterns.

By accident, I discovered the technique (concurrent family and group therapy) and its contribution to treating veterans with PTSD. My female social worker co-therapist was an integral part of the therapeutic process. Concurrent family therapy was initiated by one group member when he had reached an impasse in his marital difficulties; he requested a private session with his wife. More critical than resolving his marital conflict was the discovery that what goes on in family therapy can be processed back into the group. This feedback loop is then completed when, through feedback within the group, permission is granted for the veteran to implement corrective therapeutic intervention at home.

Over my years of clinical practice with military psychiatry, my age range of group therapy patients has been 18–30 and up to the near 80s. My most challenging case was an elderly battle-seasoned Army veteran, Paul, who had served in three wars (World War II, Korea, Vietnam). He was the only group member whose dysphoria could not be held in check. Tears would appear spontaneously and somewhat unpredictably. Of all the combat trauma he had experienced, none was more mentally and emotionally painful than the tragic events of the last major battle of World War II in the Pacific, Okinawa, one of the bloodiest, resulting in over 200,000 deaths (both military and civilian). He lived into his 80s, and this event, experienced when he was 18, haunted him for the remainder of his years. Occasionally, he would slump his lanky 6'2" frame forward, and the tears would flow as he would engage in a faraway flashback of that day when he followed an order by his commander to shoot the women, resulting in an unforgiving self-inflicted moral trauma.

At Okinawa, the U.S. Army and Marine Corps were opposed by fierce resistance from the Japanese forces. To break this initial resistance, commanders resorted to deliberate and extreme measures. Later, a soldier testified that his commander ordered his unit to shoot Okinawan women who had been passing information about the Americans to the enemy. This deliberate action was shocking; some troops refused to follow the order. Paul was a very young man then, and as sometimes happens, the young ones obey an order that is against their moral conscience, but the unconscious never forgets, and they pay a hefty price, resulting in entrenched chronic PTSD. Existential therapy for this group became a productive strategy for him to cope on a routine and pragmatic basis, getting through each day.

When combined with family therapy, group therapy provides augmented therapeutic benefits. Among these are: (1) an outlet for a controlled release of intense feelings toward others; (2) the diminishing of reluctance to identify and share inner emotional conflicts; (3) opportunities for less risk-taking in a psychologically safe environment where new behaviors may be attempted. In addition, through these efforts, the group sessions can be a catalyst for change within the respective families.

DeFazio and Pascucci (1984) correctly observed that the symptoms that tend to be most decompensating and often precipitate referrals to mental health professionals revolve around feelings of estrangement from others and the hiatus experienced by the veteran and his family.

If therapy offers lasting hope for these veterans, it must be linked to the family unit so that the veteran can use the therapeutic process as a psychological laboratory for emotional correction in his daily life experiences. In this treatment strategy, the veteran's triangular dilemma (vis-a-vis persecutor, rescuer, and victim roles) is interrupted; he is given new assumptions about himself, and only then can he surrender the victim role.

In more recent conflicts, including the Gulf War, military psychologists have increasingly employed evidence-based treatments such as cognitive behavioral therapy (CBT) and eye movement desensitization and reprocessing (EMDR). CBT is a widely used form of psychotherapy that aims to help service members identify, understand and change their patterns of thinking and behavior. This type of therapy is based on the idea that our thoughts, feelings, and behaviors are interconnected, and that by changing our thoughts, we can change our experiences and also our reactions to them. CBT has been proven effective in treating a wide range of mental health issues, including anxiety, depression, and post-traumatic stress disorder.

EMDR is a specialized form of therapy that has been found to be particularly effective in treating trauma-related disorders. This therapy involves an eye-phase treatment where the clinician instructs the patient to follow his/her finger which moves side-to-side laterally, a procedure which typically occurs as part of an eye clinic examination (a test for nystagmus). This bilateral stimulation occurs simultaneous as the patient focuses on a distressing memory, (stimulus), e.g., a word, associated with a traumatic event. In the process, the patient learns to reprocess emotional reactivity associated with trauma in a way that reduces their impact. They still can recall the memory but without as much intensity.

For Ralph, the soldier whose hand froze on a grenade, the answer to his traumatic experience and stress came years later, having met a psychologist, John Watkins, who was treating veterans from World War II with hypnotherapy techniques known as "regressive hypnosis" to help patients recall the trauma during the hypnotic session. Dr. Watkins was able to interject reinterpretation of the incident for this troubled veteran, who had no use of his right index finger. After trance induction, Dr. Watkins regressed Ralph back to the trauma scene, where he held the hand grenade but could not throw it. Dr. Watkins told him explicitly, "No, you did nothing wrong. The colonel told you not to throw the hand grenade." This technique was repeated numerous times until Ralph finally accepted this reinterpretation as the truth. From that time forward, remarkably, the veteran recovered from his paralytic index finger (which was used to activate the pin on the hand grenade).

Hypnotherapy involves using hypnosis to access the subconscious mind and promote healing or behavior change. It has been used in various therapeutic contexts, including pain management, stress reduction, and treatment of anxiety disorders. In my psychiatric treatments with veterans and active-duty personnel, I have found that hypnotherapy, combined with other treatment programs, is highly effective. Unfortunately, hypnosis and hypnotherapy have often been denigrated because of skepticism and misconceptions. Hypnotherapy is widely misunderstood by the general public as well as military personnel. Moreover, there are few trained practitioners, so it has been difficult to gauge the effectiveness of a seldom-tried treatment.

I was first intrigued by published papers on hypnotherapy in graduate school, but my direct experience did not start until I began working as a psychologist in Singapore. Then, I attended a hypnotherapy symposium taught by Dr. John Hartland, a world-renowned hypnotist, known as the "Father of Hypnosis in Britain." The symposium was attended primarily by Singapore physicians. Being hypnotized by Dr. Hartland was indelible to my initiation. This training in 1976 inspired and motivated me to further develop advanced hypnotherapy techniques.

The following year I studied hypnotherapy techniques under Professor Dr. Donald Schaefer, a Professor at the University of California, Irvine, and psychologist Dr. John Watkins. The advanced course was held in Los Angeles, California, in October 1977. Later, as an intern at the University of Kansas Medical Center, I treated a number of patients with hypnotherapy which brought attention and interest from a visiting professor from the Menninger Institute in Topeka, Kansas. He used many hours of the videotaped sessions to teach residents in training at the Menninger Institute.

I found reinterpretation and regressive techniques of hypnotherapy to be very beneficial in some instances of trauma and especially for childhood trauma when treating, for example, dissociative disorders or multiple personalities. I later used hypnotherapy with active-duty military personnel at an Army installation. I was the solo practitioner of this technique, which seemed novel to some other staff who had never seen or used it.

Hypnotherapy in the military has not been well received due to the bad press it has received over the years. That said, the use of hypnotherapy as a treatment for PTSD in the military has been explored to some extent. For example, a case study published in 2013 reported that a Vietnam War veteran with PTSD received hypnotherapy in conjunction with CBT (Scholtz, 2013). The patient reported significantly reduced PTSD symptoms and improved quality of life after treatment. The study concluded that hypnotherapy, when used as an adjunct to evidence-based therapies like CBT, could be helpful for some veterans with PTSD.

A 2007 study by David W. H. Barlow, Gary R. Elkins, and Aimee K. H. Barlow examined the use of hypnotherapy in treating PTSD in a sample of 30 veterans and emergency responders (Barlow, Elkins, and Barlow, 2007). The study found that participants who received hypnotherapy experienced significant reductions in PTSD symptoms and improvements in overall psychological functioning compared to those who received a control intervention. As a result, the authors suggested that hypnotherapy could be a useful adjunct treatment for individuals with PTSD.

Of course, the U.S. military predominantly relies on evidence-based treatments for PTSD, such as CBT, EMDR, and medication management. These approaches have been widely researched and demonstrated as effective in treating PTSD among military personnel and veterans. I would like to see a greater willingness to try alternative therapies such as hypnosis. Still, I understand that the U.S. military moves slowly and often lags behind civilian psychiatric treatments.

As research on hypnotherapy and other alternative therapies expands, it is important to continue educating mental health professionals, military personnel, and the general public about the potential benefits of these treatments. In addition, sharing the successes of case studies and clinical trials can help to dispel myths and misconceptions about hypnotherapy and encourage its integration into mainstream mental health care.

One way to promote the use of hypnotherapy in the military is through training mental health professionals within the military system. By offering specialized courses and workshops on hypnotherapy, the military can ensure that more qualified practitioners can provide this treatment option to service members.

Additionally, collaborations between military and civilian mental health professionals can facilitate the exchange of knowledge and expertise, ultimately benefiting both populations. For example, civilian mental health professionals with experience in hypnotherapy can share their expertise with military psychologists. In contrast, military psychologists can share their unique insights into service members' challenges.

Furthermore, incorporating hypnotherapy into existing mental health programs within the military can provide service members with a comprehensive range of treatment options. This integrative approach can help address the complex and multifaceted nature of PTSD and other mental health conditions prevalent among military personnel and veterans.

U.S. Military Psychiatric Treatments Compared to Other Countries

The U.S. military is one of the world's largest and best funded, enabling it to invest more resources in mental health care services for its personnel and veterans. This greater investment in resources can lead to more extensive mental health care programs, research initiatives, and access to evidence-based treatments.

As a result, the U.S. military has been at the forefront of research and development in mental health care, contributing to advancing evidence-based treatments such as CBT and EMDR. This focus on research and development has helped establish the U.S. military as a military mental health care leader. Moreover, the U.S. military has implemented comprehensive mental health care programs, such as the Army's Comprehensive Soldier Fitness (CSF) initiative and the Marine Corps Operational Stress Control and Readiness (OSCAR) program. These programs focus on early intervention, prevention, and treatment of mental health issues among military personnel.

The U.S. military often collaborates with other countries' military organizations to share best practices, conduct joint research, and develop mental health care initiatives. These collaborations and partnerships can contribute to the overall effectiveness of mental health care services in the U.S. military and other countries. Among the countries the U.S. military collaborates with include the UK, Canada, Australia, Israel, Germany, the Netherlands, New Zealand, and South Korea.

The U.S. military has benefited significantly from these collaborations with other nations. For example, the UK has a strong history of mental healthcare in their military, sharing their strategies for prevention and treatment with U.S. military counterparts. A conceptual model of a psychological health system for U.S. active-duty service members (Wang et al., 2013) highlights opportunities for improvement of the system by using more feedback mechanisms and attention to factors that influence mental health across a service member from accession to their final separation from the U.S. military by taking a systems approach.

The UK launched Improving Access to Psychological Therapies (IAPT) in 2008, considered to be the most ambitious effort to expand mental health services to engage more people with anxiety and depression in treatment, using primarily CBT. This frugal strategy differs from models of mental health care in the U.S., promoting a standardized approach and using therapists on the frontline, known as psychological well-being practitioners with one year's training in a national CBT curriculum (Priebe et al., 2021).

Canada has also provided valuable insights into trauma-informed care, while Australia has shared their expertise in suicide prevention. Overall, these collaborations can contribute to the ongoing improvement of mental healthcare services for military personnel both in the U.S. and around the world.

Each country's approach may vary depending on cultural context, available resources, and the prevalence of specific mental health issues. Collaboration and sharing best practices between nations contribute to more effective mental health care for military personnel and veterans globally, and I hope more cooperation will be the norm.

The Role of Elite Special Operations Units in Military Psychiatric Treatments

Elite special operations units like the Navy SEALs, Army Rangers, and Air Force Pararescue present unique challenges for mental health, given the coping strategies which are needed to endure and successfully complete the training. Such extreme training measures for covert missions can put operators at risk for developing post-traumatic stress symptoms. However, tight-knit unit cohesion and specialized medical care also enable innovation in psychiatric treatment tailored to their needs.

Ensuring access to mental health resources can be difficult for globally dispersed special ops teams engaged in secretive missions. Embedded unit psychologists trained in addressing operational stress can help circumvent these barriers. Telemedicine capabilities also allow remote counseling, though connectivity limits its use in austere settings.

Many elite operators hesitate to seek treatment due to stigma and pressure to maintain operational readiness. However, ongoing unit engagement with psychologists builds critical trust and encourages help-seeking when needed. Command's role in advocating for mental wellness is especially impactful with prestige units.

Novel interventions leveraging virtual reality exposure therapy show promise for elite operators who experience traumatic events. VR provides controlled treatment similar to real-world mission environments. Augmented reality delivered in vivo during training exercises could also help instill stress resilience.

Hypnotherapy may benefit select special ops patients who have developed psychological problems due to their stressful assignments which resulted in significant trauma and left them with frequent dissociative episodes. Careful assessment is needed, however, as dissociation can represent a conditioned psychological coping mechanism necessary in combat.

The insular nature of elite units promotes selective sharing of mental health approaches. More open collaboration between special ops psychologists and conventional military providers could better disseminate innovative practices. Overall, special operations communities present high yet nuanced mental health needs requiring context-specific psychiatric care built on trust and a duty-first approach. Their treatment innovations could inform the wider military.

Recent Advances

Technological advancements have led to the development of telemedicine and virtual reality exposure therapy for military personnel. Telemedicine allows mental health professionals to provide remote care to service members, increasing access to treatment for those in rural or remote areas. Virtual reality exposure therapy uses immersive virtual environments to expose patients to traumatic events in a controlled manner, helping them gradually confront and process their experiences.

Technological advancements are rapidly transforming military psychiatry. Telemedicine, wearable sensors, artificial intelligence (AI) chatbots, VR exposure therapy, and smartphone apps are enhancing access, delivery, diagnosis, and treatment. While technology is no panacea, carefully targeted solutions can augment care for service members and veterans.

The COVID-19 pandemic accelerated the shift to telepsychiatry across U.S. military treatment facilities. Virtual visits increased convenience for patients while adhering to physical distancing protocols. Telepsychiatry also reached personnel deployed abroad and those in rural areas with provider shortages. However, some patients still prefer and may benefit more from in-person care, especially when that patient requires intensive psychotherapy and enhanced therapeutic alliance.

Remote patient monitoring systems using wearable biosensors and smartphone apps can enable continuous assessment of mental health outside the clinic. Passive data, such as sleep and activity patterns and self-reported mood, can inform diagnoses and treatment plans. Yet privacy issues around biometric data collection exist.

AI chatbots are being developed for initial mental health screening and psychoeducation. Algorithms may eventually assist with treatment recommendations. However, they lack human empathy and emotional intelligence vital to psychiatry. Rigorous testing for efficacy and risks like user manipulation is critical before implementation.

VR exposure therapy shows success in treating PTSD by immersing patients in traumatic scenarios within a controlled environment. Though more research is needed, combining VR with neurofeedback may enhance outcomes. Other innovations like psychedelic medicines and transcranial stimulation (TMS) are also undergoing trials. TMS has gained considerable attention among clinicians, and efficacy appears to be reliable with both depression and PTSD patients. TMS has been FDA-cleared to treat Major Depressive Disorder since 2013.

While technology can augment military psychiatric care, human connection and trust remain paramount. Hybrid models thoughtfully integrating virtual tools, data analytics, and new modalities with in-person treatment can maximize clinical outcomes. Looking ahead, close collaboration with patients to design tech-based solutions centered on their needs is key.

John Kasich, former governor of Ohio, and William Owens (retired) have written about their concerns about America's lack of visionaries in the military and too much reliance on favorite or out-worn systems, which are now obsolete for preparing the country for rapidly changing threats. They argue that it's necessary for a paradigm shift to prioritize including new technologies in the military, e.g., artificial intelligence.

I believe we have barely peeled the onion to discover the potential use and the safeguards that must be in place with this new technology. Maybe we need a cultural shift to focus on the future to see the new strategy to be battle ready for the defense of the United States. This also applies to how we will eventually retrofit the country's present mental health treatment system with new technological advancements. AI may become an expansion of a conglomerate database for diagnosticians in the military. How this will be used will be of utmost concern for mental health providers across all branches of service and agencies. We already know the dangers of programmed diagnoses and how that system can make errors in accuracy for exceptions. Templates are helpful but can be too often a crutch or excuse not to look for answers elsewhere.

Preventative Psychiatry

Acute stress disorder (ASD) is a common psychological reaction experienced by service members exposed to extreme traumatic situations, such as combat or military sexual trauma. The condition is characterized by a rapid onset of anxiety and dissociative symptoms, including reexperiencing via nightmares, avoidance, numbing, exaggerated startle, and hypervigilance, lasting typically for one month or less. Moreover, it can be the precursor to PTSD if it continues. The longer the time between trauma exposure and treatment, the higher the risk of developing chronic PTSD. This highlights the need for early aggressive treatment of ASD to prevent PTSD, which can be lifelong and lead to many adverse physical and mental health outcomes.

Current strategies for treating acute stress reactions typically focus on psychological first aid, monitoring, and supportive counseling. Although these approaches can be effective in the short term, they do not address the underlying causes of the trauma and the specific symptoms of ASD. For example, a study by Marmar et al. (2006) found that early cognitive behavioral therapy intervention for military personnel with ASD resulted in significantly lower rates of PTSD six months after the intervention compared to those who received supportive counseling.

The potential of leveraging technology for preventative psychiatry efforts in the military is immense yet largely untapped. Developing more proactive mental health screening and intervention protocols through innovative tech solutions could transform treatment paradigms for service members.

In addition to using virtual reality and augmented reality training discussed previously, wearable biosensors are another prevention tool. Devices tracking physiological signals like heart rate variability could identify early signs of stress reactions in soldiers. This data could trigger real-time mobile interventions like breathing exercises or mindfulness sessions to mitigate distress. Machine-learning algorithms drawing on biomarker data could also predict vulnerability to conditions like PTSD.

As mentioned previously, conversational agents and AI-powered chatbots could aid prevention efforts, as could telemedicine platforms. However, there are risks in applying technology to preventative psychiatry which must be addressed. For instance, AI and algorithms used for screening or diagnosis require extreme caution given their potential for bias and inaccuracy. Proactive outreach must also avoid being perceived as intrusive or coercive by service members. And research on effectiveness should guide implementation.

With careful evidence-based deployment centered on user needs, technology tools show immense promise in transitioning the military from reactive to proactive psychiatric models. Technological innovation could enable the mass delivery of preventative interventions to build resilience and maximize mental readiness. Integrating tech-based solutions into a comprehensive prevention strategy may be key to supporting the psychological health of America's military personnel.

A New Strategy

The history and development of psychiatric treatments in the U.S. military demonstrate a continuous evolution in understanding the mental health needs of service members. As a result, the military has gained a deeper understanding of war's psychological impact on each conflict and adapted its approaches accordingly. Yet, today, while the U.S. military is committed to providing evidence-based, innovative, and accessible mental health care to its members, ensuring that those who serve their country receive the support they need and deserve, I feel there is still significant room for improvement.

As already discussed, prevention and early intervention strategies, such as resilience training and stress management, are particularly beneficial for younger soldiers to help them develop coping skills and reduce the risk of mental health issues. Nevertheless, younger soldiers may be more likely to need psychiatric treatment due to their developmental stage, lack of life experience, and exposure to combat.

In a new strategy, several factors need to be considered. First, there needs to be an even greater shift in the culture of the military and its approach to mental health. Although the military has been working to remove the stigma associated with service members declaring mental health problems, this problem still exists. It is often still present as "DON'T ASK, DON'T TELL." In addition, the perception still exists among some personnel that mental health problems are the realm of the weak and inferior.

Second, a comprehensive mental health screening program must be mandated for every service member as a tool for pre-deployment, post-deployment, and periodically during service. Third, once identified, service members with ASD should receive early aggressive treatment that addresses the specific symptoms of ASD. This should include interventions such as CBT, exposure therapy, EMDR, and hypnotherapy (when appropriate). Psychedelics (psilocybin) may hold some promise for chronic cases (Krediet et al., 2020). Still, it is too soon for any standard protocol for this. And fourth, follow-up and monitoring of service members with ASD should be conducted to ensure they have not developed PTSD.

These strategies can only be effective if they are supported 100 percent by command. This means the utmost priority is to see that no service member is excluded or exempt. Support from the military leadership, policymakers, and stakeholders is paramount for the implementation and efficacy of these measures.

Pre-deployment stress inoculation is an education program that prepares the service member by exposing them to combat scenes and introduce coping strategies for possible combat trauma. It may be a deterrent for PTSD. In addition, pre-deployment training has helped service members build resiliency and develop coping mechanisms before exposure to trauma. The U.S. military has implemented several training programs to prepare service members for the stress of deployment (Hoge et al., 2004). These programs provide education on common combat stress reactions, offer coping strategies, and emphasize the importance of building social support systems.

Additionally, some studies have suggested that social support from fellow service members and family members is crucial in reducing the risk of developing PTSD (Schnurr et al., 2001). According to this study, service members who report higher levels of social support have been shown to have lower levels of PTSD symptoms.

Providing Holistic Support for Modern Military Families

It is not only the service members themselves who would benefit from the latest evidence-based mental health therapeutic methods. As a clinical psychologist, psychiatrist, and veteran officer, I firmly believe we have an ethical responsibility to openly acknowledge the far-reaching ripple effects of extended military service on our brave service members' families. Only by doing so can we deliberately craft and proactively provide that comprehensive network of social, emotional, and practical support systems that military families desperately need to survive and hopefully thrive amid the unrelenting demands both physically and emotionally.

Military spouses and children make profound personal sacrifices alongside the uniformed service members—and the provision of resources within the military community must explicitly acknowledge that solemn reality. Providing access to robust mental health services becomes especially crucial during wartime deployments, which reliably impose unbearable stress and uncertainty on military families already weighed down by the daily sacrifices of military life. Their very survival rests upon America's collective ability and moral commitment to offer, without question or delay, all the robust emotional and practical support systems specifically tailored to address military families' unique needs. Military families are unsung heroes. Their well-being and the stability of the military family unit warrant focused attention, understanding, and tangible commitment to ongoing compassionate care.

During the extended conflicts in Iraq and Afghanistan in the first decades of the 21st century, the U.S. military admirably developed a Family Readiness Groups (FRGs) network to provide enhanced social/emotional support and critical services to service members' spouses and families throughout all deployment phases. For military families able to actively participate, FRG programs can facilitate invaluable peer bonding and provide practical resources and substantive support during prolonged periods of service member absence. However, for overburdened spouses unable to engage consistently, such support interventions can prove insufficient to meet family needs. As deployment separations grew longer and more frequent over two decades of war, more and more military families have reached their breaking point. As one weary young mother of two small children (herself still working full-time) aptly conveyed after her husband's third combat deployment overseas, "Three tours in, I still have days when I barely hold it together. I just want to hide under the bed and cry."

An Associated Press story in 2008 emphasized this tipping point had become all too common after multiple deployments. The article noted that one busy military family law firm at that time was processing the highest rate of divorce cases and family counseling referrals in over a decade. The attorneys and counselors observed time and again that the accumulation of a second or third combat deployment often represented the proverbial "final straw" for many struggling military couples:

> To leave the family for one grueling combat deployment is difficult, but the joyous reunions and relationship readjustment during reintegration leave most military families hopeful, if weathered. However, when the same service member is thrust into a second or third back-to-back combat deployment overseas, and families are threatened with yet more extended separation under perilous conditions, it's just emotionally devastating for the couples and children left behind.

This onerous scenario has been prevalent and problematic for today's young military wives—representing nearly twice the proportion compared to Vietnam- and Korea-era military spouses—who face the relentless challenge of independently providing for their family's daily needs and maintaining a semblance of household stability. At the same time, their husband serves in combat halfway around the world. For months, these women are forced to single-handedly tackle childrearing duties, household maintenance, financial and legal matters, and the constant worry of a spouse in harm's way—often while working outside the home. The resultant stress can understandably prove overwhelming. And without their partner present to reinforce boundaries, some wives report feeling ill-equipped to maintain consistent behavioral boundaries and discipline. Unresolved parent-child conflicts and family problems left to fester in the absence of the deployed father have potentially devastating consequences—not just for the family but for the service member's military unit as well.

As astutely noted by Army psychiatrist and author Simon Pincus (2001), "From a psychological perspective, it is often easier for stressed spouses and children to channel their formidable worry and grief into anger and resentment than to patiently endure the pain of repeatedly saying goodbye to their loved one departing for the dangers of combat overseas. This emotional preoccupation substantially distracts from mission focus and effectiveness." Without adequate support, spousal and child resentment over repeated deployments can manifest as acting-out behaviors, clinical depression, or even substance abuse—leading to disciplinary action jeopardizing the service member's career.

The cascading difficulties faced by military wives abandoned on the home front can also directly undermine the effectiveness of our dedicated soldiers serving overseas. The persistence of unresolved marital conflict, adolescent acting out behaviors left unchecked, financial hardship, or simply the absence of day-to-day emotional support from a spouse—these common scenarios breed potent worry and distraction from mission duties, compromising a soldier's ability to serve with undivided attention and peak performance. When forced to divert precious mental focus toward concerns about the welfare and stability of their crumbling families back home, service members naturally risk becoming less diligent, decisive, and disciplined in executing their duties. Their work productivity and leadership suffer, mission readiness declines, and risks increase in operational theaters—an outcome that serves neither families nor the military's objectives.

Realizing the outsized influence of family dynamics on military member performance underscores the urgent need for policies, programs, and a cultural shift both within the military community and throughout broader society. First, we must continue working diligently to foster a climate of genuine sensitivity, empathy, and understanding surrounding military families' unique struggles and daily sacrifices—not just superficial awareness but authentic engagement to ensure these families consistently feel included, appreciated, supported, and never forgotten regardless of where the nation's security needs take their loved ones. Beyond just words, this necessitates our collective action as communities and institutions to ensure military families receive every tangible assistance they need to survive and actively thrive.

According to retired Army colonel and military family resilience expert, Pauline Kiser, there are seven hallmarks common among the most resilient military families. These hallmarks have been identified through her extensive research and work with military families: (1) a strong familial commitment and close emotional bonds despite physical separation; (2) stable intimate relationships with at least one supportive extended family member to minimize isolation; (3) effective organization and shared leadership in clearly defined family roles; (4) a collective belief within the family in their ability to succeed together despite challenges; (5) proactive implementation of deliberate strategies and services to manage demands imposed by external stressors; (6) willingness to consistently work through problems in relationships and roles to resolve issues; (7) priority placed on actively maintaining supportive social connections in both military and civilian friend networks.

These evidence-based insights suggest numerous ways military communities, government agencies, and civilian organizations can strengthen the support framework available for military families.

As a first step, giving the military medical corps both oversight and resources to treat military families seems like a reasonable step. However, as currently configured, the U.S. military medical corps is already grappling with staff and resource shortages and is, therefore, unlikely to be charged with an even broader mandate. Unfortunately, there are no obvious ways to address the problem short of congressional intervention. Given how many other issues appear to be more urgent or essential, this area is unlikely to receive any high-level attention for quite a while.

Educational institutions can play an especially pivotal role through initiatives that cater to the unique needs of children from military families. Such programs include specialized academic counseling, peer mentorship led by students who grew up in military families, targeted inclusion efforts within the school community, and staff training for identifying signs of deployment-related distress. Students' issues and mental health needs must be addressed before they escalate.

Moreover, civilian employers in the private and public sectors can make an enormous positive difference by implementing family-friendly policies that tangibly support military spouses juggling a career with deployment disruptions—for example, allowing flexible telework options and temporary duty reassignments to maintain employment throughout frequent relocations. Providing on-site childcare, family counseling benefits, veteran hiring initiatives, and veteran employee mentors fosters inclusion.

Additionally, community-led nonprofit organizations nationwide provide invaluable services to fill support gaps for military families: hosting recreational activities and youth camps, offering deployment readiness programs, providing childcare assistance and mom support groups, organizing care packages, and pre-deployment family events, just to name a few examples. Local initiatives like these are powerful ways civilian communities can build a sense of belonging and community for transient military families while offering consistent emotional support and practical help during deployments.

And finally, legislative action at state and federal levels of government remains key to enacting policies that meaningfully improve the comprehensive support framework for modern military families—for example, extending access to mental health care services, increasing options for exceptional education regardless of duty station location, providing temporary financial assistance to struggling families, and reforming outdated tax and legal policies not designed for a mobile all-volunteer force. Managed well, government policy can still be the tide that lifts all ships.

But ultimately, successfully caring for military families remains a solemn shared responsibility not just for the various organizations mentioned above but for every American citizen. Their unique challenges certainly set them apart in some respects. Still, the solutions begin with the nation's collective will, shared values of service and sacrifice, and the individual actions citizens can contribute through volunteerism, mentorship, acts of kindness, and just taking the time to listen and understand. By embracing that mindset of outreach, acknowledging the hurdles these families face, and taking purposeful steps to provide tangible, holistic support systems, I firmly believe we have it within our power to build a new era of understanding and a more inclusive, compassionate environment for all U.S. military families—one they truly deserve.

CHAPTER 10

Centralizing the Military Health System to Better Serve All Ages

As we age, our medical needs evolve and become more complex. Nowhere is this truer than in the military, where service members are susceptible to unique health issues that arise from their demanding jobs. Younger recruits tend to have more acute injury-related needs, while older veterans deal with the long-term physical and mental toll of service through conditions such as chronic pain, PTSD, and suicide risk. In recent years, the military has struggled to provide adequate care across all branches and stages of service members' careers.

Turf wars between the fragmented military health services have led to gaps in care, endangering troops of all ages. Bringing together the military's fragmented health systems into one integrated Military Health System (MHS) would better serve service members' diverse and changing medical needs throughout their careers, from recruit to veteran.

Deadly Turf Wars and Inadequate Care

A service member, MG, began experiencing severe symptoms and was diagnosed with a rare and potentially life-threatening medical condition. His attending physician recommended immediate treatment from a military doctor specialized in the relevant field. Unfortunately, the sought-after specialist was stationed at a different military installation.

Upon receiving the treating physician's request to have the specialist flown in or to send MG to the specialist's location, the commander denied the request. Why? Of course, he did not need to give anyone a reason or justification, but it was well known within the corps that the commander often exhibited paranoid behavior. Somewhere in the man's addled brain was the thought that sending the soldier to a specialist or bringing a specialist in would undermine his authority. It became a significant issue where preventable mismanagement led to consequences that placed MG's health and life at risk.

Fortunately, irrational behavior among top medical personnel is not typical, but turf battles are a daily occurrence. Still, MG's case highlights the effects of turf protection and draws attention to possible shortcomings in the organization and management of military medical care. In denying MG immediate access to a qualified doctor, the involved commander jeopardized the service member's health and raised questions about the military's ability to accommodate complex medical needs and coordinate across different military installations.

During the Iraq War, a U.S. Army general refused to send a cardiologist to a base where heart issues were common but cardiology services were lacking. The general claimed there was no cardiology ward to justify the specialist. In reality, having a cardiologist on staff could have enabled triaging acute cardiology cases. However, the general failed to grasp the life-saving necessity of a cardiologist or simply didn't care. Either way, his decision stood firm: request denied. This example harkened back to my deployment in 2008, which I discussed at the start of this book. After I arrived in Germany, the required screening procedure by the medical corps in Landstuhl brought attention to my cardiac status (a base rate of 37 and skipped beats). I was then ordered to remain in Germany for active duty. However, the Army would not allow me to serve in a theater without access to a field hospital, which could provide appropriate medical care for a possible cardiac event necessitating a surgical procedure. The logical decision would have been for the Army medical and surgical corps to implant a pacemaker so that I could be sent anywhere. Of course, soldiers aren't supposed to have pacemakers, so that idea could never get off the ground.

I have also had professional experience of this issue. When I was on active duty at the U.S. Army medical center in Heidelberg, Germany, during the Iraq War, just two days before the completion of my tour of duty, the DCCS (Deputy Chief of Clinical Services) in Würzburg was in dire need of a psychiatrist. Two of his soldiers had been admitted into a German neurological inpatient facility in Bamberg. The admitting German psychiatrist insisted that their care be turned over to a U.S. Army psychiatrist. I agreed to volunteer to fill this emergent request because the U.S. Army medical clinic in Würzburg had just lost its only psychiatrist. The DCCS recommended that I go to Bamberg. He also needed me to support the mission requirements for the pre-deployment of the 173rd Airborne Battalion.

Unfortunately, an acute shortage of a psychiatrist in Bamberg and Würzburg, with no one with my medical training to assess service members in his unit who needed to be cleared for battle readiness, i.e., a crucial need to be psychiatrically cleared for unrestricted duty. Such considerations are not trivial. If a mentally unfit soldier, the proverbial loose cannon, is sent into a theater, such a decision can easily result in casualties.

Despite the above, the DCCS in Heidelberg refused to lend me to the Bamberg facility for service duty. Why? Did the Heidelberg DCCS want to protect his turf? Did it matter that the lack of psychiatric support at a nearby military facility was causing undue stress and hardship on colleagues and soldiers? Apparently not. Lending me out was seen as a loss of resources. Here is where ego and a position of control enter a power struggle. And since I was in his "house," he had rightful ownership. Rank has its privilege, but so does position, and both DCCSs were colonels and technically equals. Request denied.

The issue didn't end there, however. Without my knowledge, another back-channel attempt was made to transfer me to Bamberg. On the last day of my active-duty assignment in Heidelberg, I was on the phone with a sergeant, then I heard the commander's (chief of psychiatry) voice: "It's not going to cost Human Resources in St. Louis anything. It comes out of the Würzburg budget." The commander's secretary gave me the name of "Major V" as "a person with many skills and know-how." Later in the afternoon, Major V called me. "Okay, we got your orders approved. You're going to Bamberg."

Two hours later, I received another call from her. "You're not going anywhere. Someone has placed a block on your orders. I have connections in high places, and someone must have been upset that I had gone around or over them."

During wartime, especially, one might hope that turf battles would defer to more urgent issues of helping the overall cause. Leaders on the ground who control limited resources should be willing to share those resources with other groups, divisions, and battalions. And yet, such is not always the case.

For example, the triage concept within hospitals—namely, treating the most severely wounded who may yet recover and ignoring the ones who won't make it—does not extend to other parts of military organizations. A commanding officer might hear pleas from different divisions— "You have five psychiatrists, and we have none. Surely, you can spare us at least one"—and be unmoved. In such a case, where there is no one to examine an 18-year-old tank gunner, it falls on the shoulders of military doctors whose entire training in psychiatry usually consists of a three-week rotation through a hospital. Are they qualified to decide if someone's symptoms are debilitating and too great a risk for deployment? The answer is they are decidedly not trained for psychiatric screening and treating psychiatric disorders.

Situations like these are all too common within the fragmented structure of today's military health system. During wartime especially, turf wars should yield to the greater mission. On the ground, commanders must be willing to share limited resources across divisions when necessary. Just as hospital triage privileges those most in need, so too should military medicine. A commander petitioned to lend one of five psychiatrists to an installation with none should rise to the call. After all, deploying unfit personnel can risk lives. But under separate chains of command, such pleas often go unheeded.

I believe that the structure of the medical corps in the U.S. is partly to blame. The corps is a separate military branch, with subdivisions for the Army, Navy, and Air Force. The Army Medical Department (AMEDD) comprises officers and enlisted personnel and is responsible for providing a comprehensive range of medical services, including preventive care, surgical operations, and mental health services to members of the U.S. Army. The Air Force Medical Service (AFMS) provides medical services to Air Force personnel, their families, and wounded warriors in aviation and space contexts. The Navy Bureau of Medicine and Surgery (BUMED) provides medical and dental services to naval and Marine Corps personnel. The Public Health Service treats the Coast Guard. Each branch has its unique structure, and all are responsible for providing medical care to military personnel and their families.

Each medical corps exists as a complete entity unto itself, servicing the needs of the branch as if the other branches did not exist. It is as if they exist as three separate health maintenance organizations (HMOs). For example, an Air Force pilot who might benefit from a specialist who works for the Navy is out of luck. They treat their own, even though they are technically all on the same team.

The divided American model likely evolved from the massive scale of U.S. global operations and how medical units developed independently. But in modern times, this system has become outdated and inefficient. The rigid separation of medical branches cannot optimally serve the evolving needs of today's military. The specialists, e.g., dentists, nurses, social workers, psychologists, and surgeons require an excess of medical personnel to support military operations worldwide.

This bureaucratic tangle of disjointed services is atypical among international forces. Few countries other than the U.S. have an Armed Forces medical corps, e.g., Syria, Ukraine, Azerbaijan, and Belarus. Many countries without a formally recognized medical corps have various military doctors and medical staff who often support the frontline troops. Some medical personnel may also be trained in rudimentary battlefield medicine and integrated into the military. For example, Great Britain and Canada have integrated medical personnel into their armies, navies, and air forces.

The U.S. Army, Air Force, and Navy each have their unique approach to medical services that ensure the well-being and readiness of their respective personnel. However, with the changing nature of warfare and the emergence of new medical technologies, the question arises whether all branches of medical services should exist under one umbrella.

The Way Forward: A Modern, Integrated Military Health System

There are apparent benefits of a unified medical service for all military branches. A unified system would eradicate the inefficiencies in the three individual systems, resulting in significant cost savings as one could decrease the size of administrative staff and transfer resources from the areas where they are underused. With a unified system, there would be ease of coordinated care, leading to enhanced continuity of care and exchange of information between medical specialists. Sharing resources and collaboration between military branches would improve access to cutting-edge medical technologies and research. The sharing of knowledge and resources ultimately would lead to the development of improved medical treatments throughout the system.

What would an integrated Military Health System look like? Firstly, it would be centrally managed under the Secretary of Defense to provide consistent policies and transparency. Specialists could be seamlessly transferred anywhere required, with streamlined coordination among hospitals. Cutting redundant administrative roles would allow for investment in strengthened security and advanced technology. Information and research would be jointly leveraged to unlock innovation.

Far from diminishing military doctors' importance, a unified MHS would empower them to better fulfill their primary duty of protecting troops' lives. Critically, centralization would enable better continuity of care across a service member's full career. Entering as a fit young recruit, a soldier may serve for decades, taking him into advanced age. As mentioned previously, the physical and mental toll of service often manifests in complex health needs later in life. An integrated MHS would foster expertise in veteran care and enable smooth transitions for aging patients.

No longer would a veteran requiring specialty care face roadblocks to seeing the right provider. Some skeptics may resist the perceived loss of autonomy and prestige. But in truth, united under a common purpose, military health providers would gain strength through collaboration.

By serving all military members across the lifespan, the MHS could identify health patterns that manifest over time and use those insights to optimize care. Younger soldiers tend to be affected more by acute injuries, substance abuse issues, and mental health crises, while older veterans experience higher chronic pain, cancer, heart disease, and suicide risk. With integrated data and expertise, the MHS could tailor prevention and treatment for the unique needs that emerge at each stage of military service.

Ultimately, a modernized MHS upholding a sacred obligation to safeguard the well-being of all who serve would make for a stronger fighting force. When lives are on the line, partisan divisions have no place in military medicine. Integrated care would mean swifter diagnosis, more robust treatment, and faster recoveries for ill and injured service members across every age and branch. And by caring for soldiers over the full arc of their careers, the MHS could fulfill its mission to keep troops in peak fighting condition from the moment they enlist until the day they retire.

Still, I acknowledge, with respect to the status quo of multiple health services, nothing is likely to change for a very long time. I learned early on in my military career, as was made apparent to me during my officer basic training program, the Army does what it likes, when it wants, and no one is allowed to buck the system. The reason why consolidation of redundant assets currently looks impossible is because doing so would mean that some people in power would lose control over assets they've had in their domain for decades. They will assert, "If it ain't broke, don't fix it," but the sad reality is that such leaders don't understand that the current fragmented system is entirely broken and that fixing it would solve many problems and improve lives.

In a 2022 interview, a Vietnam-era Army surgeon, LTC Crile Doscher, offered candid comments about this debate: "I think there's something about the rank and having control and power over your little bailiwick that sometimes people are unwilling to be flexible. And they're not willing to see themselves having diminished strength or diminished prominence in their position."

In the U.S.'s currently configured armed services rank is at times more important than logic. Soldiers are trained to carry out orders without question. The person in charge does not have to answer to a higher authority unless something goes wrong.

This rigid command structure can enable the troubling turf wars and irrational decision-making described in this chapter. When commanders make choices based on protecting their own resources and egos rather than the greater good, those beneath them suffer.

Yet there are hopeful signs this culture may slowly be shifting. In recent years, the armed forces have emphasized concepts like servant leadership, where officers focus on supporting and empowering those under their command rather than simply issuing top-down orders. There is also increased acknowledgment of the need to destigmatize mental health issues and provide more holistic care for both physical and emotional well-being.

Real change takes time. But the first step is acknowledging where systems have failed service members in the past and envisioning how to build a military health system capable of serving all who have sacrificed for their country. Centralizing care under the banner of the MHS would not solve every problem overnight. However, it would be a crucial move toward placing logic and patients over egos and turf wars.

With a unified health system, the needs of individual service members across every stage of their careers will finally come first. We owe this commitment to past, present, and future generations who have put service before self. It is no exaggeration to say that lives are on the line. The time has come to honor our solemn promise to care for all who shall have borne the battle. No longer can we allow rank and siloed interests to endanger those who defend the nation.

CHAPTER 11

Technology and a Reimagined Military with No Age Barriers

Radical shifts in warfare tactics and practices are becoming manifest as technology undergoes rapid evolution. As we witness the profound impacts of innovations such as cyber technology and unmanned aircraft systems—evidenced in real-time through the ongoing Ukrainian conflict—we also see the dawning of a new warfare epoch. This paradigm shift questions the long-held norm of young soldiers risking their lives on the frontlines, potentially evolving toward a technologically advanced and safer mode of warfare.

The digital era has seen an upsurge of robotic technology across diverse sectors, with the military no exception. Robots, like the "Robot Dog" developed by the U.S. military, enhance operational capabilities by assuming roles considered too risky, laborious, or complex for human personnel. Functioning beyond the limitations of human vulnerability, these machines can execute tasks that include but are not limited to intelligence gathering, surveillance, reconnaissance, and defusing explosive devices. They leverage their ability to withstand high-risk environments to mitigate threats to human personnel.

Robot Dog, designed to resemble a dog, is a crucial player in this landscape. Its ability to navigate harsh terrains, bear substantial loads, and detect hazards allows it to scout, deliver supplies, and even conduct surveillance through its integrated sensors and cameras. The constant technological advancements are likely to expand the role of robots in the military, offering valuable support in critical operations, thus redefining the traditional concept of military operations.

Unmanned aircraft systems, commonly known as drones, present another game-changing innovation. Operated remotely from secure command centers, drones reduce the risk to human pilots, executing precision strikes over vast areas and revolutionizing air operations. Yet, this advancement also invites new challenges—ethical dilemmas related to drone warfare, accountability issues, and the psychological impact on remote operators distanced from the physical battlefield realities.

Similarly, cyber technology has emerged as a vital tool in military defense systems. It transforms reactive strategies into proactive defenses by enabling real-time threat detection and responses. However, this new warfare domain brings threats, such as potential cyberattacks from non-state actors and the complexities of tracing these attacks back to their sources.

A further layer of complexity is added by AI, which has made considerable inroads into military applications. From reconnaissance and surveillance to direct combat roles, AI offers enhanced efficiency and precision while decreasing risk to human life. Significantly, these technologies can potentially facilitate the participation of individuals beyond the conventional military age, allowing them to contribute strategic insights and benefit from their accumulated life experiences.

These technological advancements may significantly impact age restrictions within the U.S. military. As the nature of military roles evolves toward remote operation, strategy, and cyber defense, the age-associated attribute of physical prowess might become less essential. Conversely, experience, strategic insight, and mature judgment—attributes generally associated with age—may gain prominence. This evolution might lead to a reevaluation or even elimination of the current age limitations in the U.S. military, thus expanding the demographics of those serving their nation.

Notwithstanding, integrating AI and robotics into military operations poses complex ethical dilemmas. The boundaries of AI autonomy and the potential misuse of autonomous weaponry raise urgent questions, underscoring the need for careful reassessment of ethical and strategic frameworks.

As we project into the future, it is unequivocal that military operations will increasingly hinge on these technological advancements. While these innovations offer opportunities to reduce human risk and augment operational efficiency, they necessitate a reassessment of traditional warfare notions. The need for informed, thoughtful discourse on technology's evolving role in modern warfare is paramount in this technology-driven era. As boots-on-the-ground operations continue to be necessary, the soldier's role is being redefined, paving the way for a more age-diverse military force ready to navigate the challenges of the 21st century.

In a 2023 interview, Vietnam War veteran and author John Musgrave offered caution: "Yes, they [drones and robots] do help assist us. But that didn't help us in Mogadishu, Beirut, Afghanistan, Iraq, or Syria, because you still need boots on the ground. Somebody's got to run those machines, and they can't all be run from a parking lot in Phoenix, Arizona."

The military has always been a revered institution that values strength, discipline, and resilience. It is paramount for any military force to be at its optimal physical and mental strength. Hence, exploring the benefits and challenges of having an older military force is necessary.

One of the potential benefits of having an older military force is the wealth of experience and wisdom they bring to the table. Unlike younger troops who may lack the expertise and decision-making prowess, more senior military personnel have a deeper understanding of humanity and conflicts. Their years of service within the military, combined with life experience, can shape their decision-making capabilities, allowing them to make better and more informed decisions. Consider, for example, medical specialists in their early-to-mid 40s; they are at the top of their game with skill and experience when the military refuses to allow them to serve (the arbitrary 43-year-old cutoff).

Furthermore, as soldiers age, they tend to have fewer responsibilities outside their careers, unlike their younger counterparts, who may have younger families and social distractions. This advantage allows them to be more focused and committed to their military duties, thus making them more efficient.

However, there are also potential challenges with having an older military force. One significant challenge is physical fitness, as older soldiers may be more susceptible to injuries and physical decline. Nevertheless, appropriate accommodations can be established to ensure they can still perform their duties optimally. Consider the developing technology through cybernetics (communication and automatic control systems) and remote learning. The future landscape of the military will bring dramatic changes in how it functions. Remote administration of duties will change the physical requirements, challenging the senior service members to keep up. There are many examples of specialists, such as radiologists, who now analyze images via Internet media from anywhere in the world. Thus, less physical demand and more efficiency are the mantras of the future.

While the use of military drones in war has been lauded for reducing the risks to soldiers on the ground, it has been shown to significantly impact the mental health of those who operate these remote weapons. Despite the physical distance from targets, drone operators are still exposed to their actions' gruesome and violent aftermath. This exposure can lead to feelings of guilt, shame, and trauma, which can manifest as PTSD. The unpredictable and ever-changing nature of war and the high-pressure environment of operating military drones create the perfect storm for mental distress among operators and other support staff. The mental health impacts of operating military drones have been well documented, with studies showing an increased incidence of depression, anxiety, and PTSD among these personnel.

An article by Dave Philipps, "The Unseen Scars of Those Who Kill Via Remote Control," published in the *New York Times*, April 15, 2022, addressed concerns for the extreme psychological trauma endured by drone crews, "launched more missiles and killed more people than nearly anyone else in the military in the past decade". He highlighted unrelenting stress for former crew members which accounted for incidences of alcoholism, divorce and attempted suicide, quoting former drone sensor operator Neal Scheuneman, "People often think that this job is going to be like a video game, and I have to warn them, there is no reset button."

A recent study of PTSD and the psychological impact on drone operators published in the *Industrial Psychiatry Journal* by Rajiv Kumar Saini et al. (October 30, 2021) revealed the incidence of PTSD among USAF drone operators was as high as 18 percent. One plausible explanation is the absence of group support or shared accountability for a collective rationale endorsed by battle buddies.

The military must take steps to address the mental health impacts of drone warfare. By recognizing and addressing these issues, we can better support service members and ensure they receive the care and support they need to lead healthy and fulfilling lives. Using tried and proven therapeutic strategies to minimize and reduce acute combat stress (e.g., disengage, debrief, decompress) can help personnel process the exposure trauma early on.

Another challenge concerns military culture, as younger troops may view older service members as outdated and past their prime. This view can create a divide among units and stifle innovation and progress. But through cooperation and respect for the unique contributions of each individual regardless of age, this difficulty can be minimized.

As advancements in telecommunications technology continue to alter how we work, there has been a growing discussion about its potential impact on the nature of war. While certain aspects of combat will never be conducted with the aid of teleconferencing platforms like Zoom, it is becoming increasingly evident that modern warfare is becoming more decentralized.

One of the critical advantages of teleworking in military operations is its ability to enable commanders to delegate tasks and make decisions more efficiently. Military leaders can quickly assess multiple scenarios and make informed decisions using real-time data analysis and communication tools. This level of decentralization can also provide a more agile and responsive strategic approach, enabling troops to react more quickly to changing circumstances on the battlefield.

However, it is worth noting that there are limitations to using telework in combat. Crucial elements such as weapons handling, marksmanship, physical endurance, and resilience are difficult to train remotely. And while telework can provide generals with valuable situational awareness, it can never replace the value of face-to-face interactions between leaders and their troops.

Ultimately, while telework may be changing the nature of combat by making military operations more decentralized, it should be considered a supplementary tool rather than a replacement for traditional training and command control forms.

The advent of other technological advancements (such as AI) presents many possibilities for implementing it in decision-making and further developing a skill set for essential and successful military operations.

Integrating AI in the Decision-Making Process

AI is revolutionizing various industries by augmenting decision-making processes. Integrating AI in military decision-making offers several advantages. Firstly, AI systems have the potential to process massive amounts of data at incredible speeds, enabling timely situational awareness. By assimilating large volumes of information from multiple sources, AI can provide commanders with a comprehensive and accurate understanding of complex operational environments. This technology can also offer an opportunity for senior-age, even elderly individuals who are experienced in various careers and specialties with a depth of knowledge and wisdom, whom would be able to contribute as a resource of assistance for this technology; a resource which our leaders should not ignore.

AI can also enhance strategic planning by analyzing historical data, identifying patterns, and generating insights. This analysis enables military planners to make data-driven decisions that optimize resource allocation, mission planning, and risk assessment. Additionally, AI can assist in simulating various scenarios, allowing military strategists to explore potential outcomes and devise effective strategies accordingly.

Furthermore, AI can automate specific tasks, allowing human operators to focus on more complex and critical decision-making aspects. Algorithms can assist in threat detection, analyzing satellite imagery, or monitoring communication channels, thus enhancing overall situational awareness and information gathering.

Despite its potential, integrating AI into military decision-making processes entails certain risks. Firstly, reliance on AI systems may introduce vulnerabilities in terms of cybersecurity. As these systems become pivotal in decision-making, adversaries may target them with sophisticated cyber-attacks, potentially disrupting or influencing operations.

Moreover, there is a concern regarding the ethical implications of AI deployment in military decisions. The use of AI raises questions about accountability and human oversight, as automated systems may lack the ability to explain the rationale behind their choices. Ensuring that AI systems adhere to human-defined rules and values is crucial to avoid unintended consequences or violations of international laws.

Furthermore, there is a risk of over-reliance on AI, potentially eroding human judgment and intuition. Safeguards must be in place to prevent blind trust in AI systems, as commanders and operators should retain the ability to evaluate AI-generated information and insights critically.

Technological Training and Military Education: Adaptation for Advanced Warfare

Within the evolving landscape of warfare, the relentless advancement of technology has significant import and implications for training and education. To effectively prepare service members for the challenges of this new, technologically advanced warfare, a range of changes in training approaches and educational strategies are necessary.

Undoubtedly, the modern battlefield demands soldiers to possess a diverse array of technical competencies. Soldiers must now be proficient in many technological disciplines to augment traditional combat skills. Mastery of specialized strategies such as cyber warfare, unmanned systems, artificial intelligence, and data analytics has become essential. Understanding these advancements and their implications is paramount to ensuring military success and minimizing vulnerabilities.

Training and education should adopt a multifaceted approach to cultivate these new skills effectively. Firstly, the integration of emerging technologies into training scenarios is crucial. Simulated environments should closely resemble real-world conditions to allow service members to acquire an acute understanding of the hands-on technologies they will employ. Personnel can immerse themselves in viable scenarios to accelerate their learning and adaptability using virtual, augmented, and advanced computer simulators.

Collaborative learning environments can also be pivotal in cultivating the required skill sets. Creating platforms where service members can exchange knowledge, tactics, and solutions will enhance their experience in collaboration within a technologically complex battlefield. Collective problem-solving and information-sharing can galvanize the dynamic that must be practiced, ensuring soldiers are well equipped to leverage technological advancement challenges.

Furthermore, educational programs should emphasize the development of critical thinking and adaptability. Service members must possess the ability to quickly comprehend and assess technological innovations and, at the same time, interpret their strengths, limitations, and potential vulnerabilities. Fostering an environment that encourages relentless curiosity and analytical thinking will enable soldiers to grasp the intricacies of emerging technologies more effectively.

To bridge the gap between theoretical knowledge and practical application, hands-on experiences must be central to military education. Muscle memory, fine-tuning their decision-making skills, and enhancing their situational awareness in stressful/high-pressure environments will be paramount as they acquire mastery and adaptation for future real-time, live operations.

Moreover, continuous training and education must be ingrained into military culture. As rapidly advancing technology continues to reshape warfare, it is essential to have a mindset of perpetual learning. Encouraging soldiers to update their skills and knowledge constantly promotes readiness and cultivates a culture of adaptability within the military.

The Shifting Physical Demands of Warfare in the Digital Age

Throughout history, military forces have heavily relied on the physical vitality of youth to endure the rigors of combat. However, the accelerating digitization of warfare threatens to disrupt this longstanding dependency. Although there are others who with conviction state that we will always need "boots on the ground." As weapons technology evolves in complexity, the most valued military skills are shifting from sheer physical prowess to intellectual aptitude and technological fluency. Consequently, the modern battlefield will likely reduce reliance on youthful vigor while elevating older service members' experience and knowledge contributions.

A prime example of this paradigm shift is the rapid rise of drone warfare. Operating unmanned aerial vehicles (UAVs) to strike targets remotely requires specialized training and skill sets unrelated to physical strength or endurance. While piloting experience remains beneficial, the role demands sharp situational analysis, shrewd decision-making, and proficiency with complex control interfaces. These cognitive capabilities tend to improve with age as seasoned pilots accumulate knowledge and pattern-recognition abilities over years of service. Of course, maintaining cognitive fitness is essential, as with all skill sets. But older drone operators can utilize their veteran insights to execute missions as effectively, if not more so, than their younger counterparts.

The growing prominence of cyber-warfare platforms also favors the intellectual strengths of maturity over youthful reflexes or stamina. Again, manipulating these systems necessitates extensive, specialized training beyond physical fitness. Rapidly evolving threats in the digital battlefield demand sharp critical thinking, nuanced discretion, and strategic prudence. Seasoned cyber warriors can leverage their veteran experience in threat assessment, defense-system management, and global cyber-terrain mapping. Younger cyber soldiers may respond quicker, but their older peers retain the contextual judgment and complex reasoning vital for cyber dominance.

Artificial intelligence and autonomous technologies will reduce reliance on human speed or vigor. As algorithms surpass biological limitations, seasoned veterans can operate advanced systems through oversight and guidance rather than direct physical manipulation. The technology allows older service members to apply their accumulated knowledge in training artificial agents and maximizing human–machine coordination. With AI handling kinetic duties once reserved for youthful soldiers, the importance of intellectual leadership supersedes sheer response times or stamina.

Some Special Forces missions will continue requiring prime physical fitness, such as special reconnaissance operations or hostage rescues. But these specialized roles comprise a diminishing fraction of modern military operations. The expanding scope of technological warfare means that cognitive capabilities take precedence over physical talents in terms of requirements.

Furthermore, telemedical resources can help extend the healthy service duration of older soldiers. Cutting-edge treatments, prosthetic aids, and performance-enhancement technologies enable veterans to maintain combat effectiveness well past ages traditionally considered unfit for duty. Remote monitoring and rapid response trauma care also preserve lives on the battlefield that would have perished in prior eras. So, while physical longevity remains limited, advanced medicine preserves capability despite age-related frailty.

Some argue that younger minds better adapt to rapidly evolving technologies, possessing malleable brains and digital native instincts. But neuroplasticity (the ability of neural networks in the brain to undergo change through growth) persists through life, and accumulated experience confers learning advantages that can offset youthful flexibility. With proper training programs emphasizing adaptability, older service members can readily integrate new technical systems and methodologies. Lifelong learning is critical, but the intellect of veterans stays sharp through continued growth and mental challenge.

Keeping all soldiers physically and mentally fit remains essential for operational readiness. But the accelerating complexity of modern warfare places greater emphasis on knowledge and judgment. As technology redefines battle, youthful vigor holds diminished utility compared to learned expertise. While physical standards must persist, intellectual acumen represents the deadlier weapon. Ultimately, integrated forces allowing qualified individuals to serve irrespective of age best support the national defense. Military institutions can cultivate a formidable amalgam of wisdom and strength by embracing this reality.

Conclusion

And so, in my later years, when by all conventions I could have been contemplating a restful retirement, I willingly embarked upon an entirely new chapter in life on my terms. Despite the adversity and challenges thrown in my path, I emerged from that crucible stronger and more committed than ever to living by my principles and upholding the ideals I believed in. I learned through hard experience that chronological age means nothing when it comes to one's capacity to effect change and make a meaningful difference in this world.

Though I may have been older in years than many of my peers, I stood tall beside them, straight back and sound in spirit. My long-life experience granted me resilience, while my enduring determination served as its testimony. I aimed to share the hard-earned lessons from my journey with the younger generation walking the same difficult road. I was there to serve to the fullest, to impart whatever wisdom I could, and to continue contributing to the Army's betterment in whatever small ways remained possible. Though by any measure, I may have been in my own "twilight years," I felt more alive and driven than ever, actively seeking out new challenges rather than withdrawing from the world. I am sincerely grateful for the resilience and indomitable strength that my age granted me in service to my country.

And here I stand before you, once a defiant civilian psychiatrist, transformed by adversity into a commissioned Army officer, head held high in the face of fierce travail. In confronting those past trials, I discovered fortitude and resilience within myself that I never knew existed. And later in life, when I had ample reason to become jaded, I instead found renewed purpose, strong in the conviction that integrity, stability, and hope must prevail over capricious power. I am living proof that these values can sustain and strengthen us, no matter the forces allied against them. Ultimately, I am simply a man who committed his life to guiding others out of darkness—a duty ever worth fighting for.

These lessons of moral courage and finding light amid darkness are not unique to my story. I hope that by sharing my experiences openly, others battling injustice may take solace and inspiration, knowing they do not stand alone. I will remain eternally grateful for the opportunity to impart whatever small measure of hope or direction I can offer fellow travelers navigating difficult times.

The Army taught me many valuable lessons over the years, but perhaps most vital was the hard-won realization that a good soldier's true compass must always point toward humanity, integrity, and moral conscience—upholding those cardinal values in every action taken. Although strong character is ideally formed early in life, there is no denying my age's instrumental role in shaping the course and outcome of this ordeal.

Time grants us not merely the repetitive revolutions of the calendar but the gradual accretion of experiences weathered, insights wrested from adversities overcome, and hard-earned wisdom ringed around the solid core of our beliefs. It equips us with emotional resilience, a psychological armor shielding us from the relentless arrows of outrageous misfortune. When linked arm-in-arm with moral courage, such stability can help a person navigate through places dark and tangled with far greater agency, emerging intact and even more whole.

There is, however, a delicate dance always at play between the quantitative passage of time and those introspective changes wrought within. It's not simply reaching some arbitrarily higher number of years lived that instills such virtues; rather, it's what we choose to do with that time—how we cultivate and marshal those resources within ourselves. I do not doubt that even if I had faced a similar crisis some decades earlier while still loyal to the Army, my actions would have hewed closely to the same principles. My essential character, formed gradually through some elusive alchemy of innate disposition, upbringing, and the willful choices I made when faced with adversity, would have guided me unerringly, as a compass guides an imperiled traveler lost in the wilderness.

In the final analysis, character and the long maturation process are inextricably interwoven into the tapestry of our fleeting lives. We are continuously molded by our experiences, even as we mold our reactions to those tests of adversity. In this ever-evolving dance across the years, the number of candles on the cake does not define a person. Rather, age refines us—hones our character, burnishes our spirit, and tempers us into finer versions of our best selves. It steels us for the challenges yet to come.

And so, as I reflect upon the circuitous route of my journey, I am reminded that while we cannot choose the obstacles strewn across our path, we can always choose how to surmount them. We can wield the sword of unflinching integrity, gird ourselves in the armor of resilience, and march ahead along the steep but righteous path. These are the true hallmarks of character, the core elements comprising who we are at our deepest levels, and they remain constant as a fixed star—unwavering, no matter our phase of life when trials befall us.

In my battle within the larger war, the wisdom of age served as an invaluable ally rather than the prime mover of my actions and reactions. It was a critical asset among many in my arsenal, bolstering my resolve when besieged from all sides. But the fundamental force which guided me, the unwavering light ever before my eyes, was my character—the bedrock foundation formed in youth but reinforced across decades of personal growth and understanding.

Throughout this book, I have emphasized the longstanding tendency of military institutions to prize the purported virtues of youth above all else when filling their enlisted ranks. The heady combination of naiveté and sheer vitality which mark the adolescent years seems to create an ideal mold for training young people to follow orders unquestioningly and hurl themselves into the line of fire when told, even if it results in near-certain annihilation. However, those traits should never be blithely mistaken as some magical formula for producing gallant, successful soldiers.

There is no doubt that the willingness of young men and women to perform audacious acts in the heat of battle, risking life and limb, has decided the outcome of many conflicts throughout history. But the actual costs of those experiences are not tallied at the moment; they ripple outward through time, subtly affecting whole communities and societies in deep, unfathomable ways. As the philosopher Ralph Waldo Emerson once wrote, "A hero is no braver than an ordinary man, but he is brave five minutes longer." It does not diminish their noble sacrifices to acknowledge the influence such trauma has upon developing minds which must bear the consequences for decades after surviving the fight.

There are no straightforward solutions and no easy answers to this complex dynamic. The potential ramifications of overhauling long-standing military recruitment and deployment policies are vast, systemic issues far beyond any one person's ability to dictate. However, within that intricate equation, the arbitrary age limitations which most global armed forces have rigidly upheld for so long do warrant thoughtful reconsideration. Perhaps the most constructive action is to approach the topic as objectively as possible, promoting reasoned dialogue and debate aimed at greater nuance.

I hope this book can help catalyze a nuanced conversation regarding age and military service. It seems we are long overdue for a reappraisal of such entrenched traditions in light of modern realities and evolving moral sensibilities. We must carefully weigh the seeming benefits against unintended costs, acknowledging that these policies profoundly impact individuals and our wider civilization.

With an enlightened approach, such discourse may encourage subtle shifts toward a more flexible, holistic, and ethical approach to recruitment and deployment—one that focuses on nurturing an adaptable fighting force while recognizing that invaluable skills, wisdom, and talents flow across the entire spectrum of ages if given a chance. After all, every society must ultimately be judged on how it treats its most vulnerable members. In this context, how we support and protect our youth during conflicts, measuring our actions against the highest collective ideals of humanity, remains the truest test of our character.

By opening the door to constructive dialogue and honest self-examination, I hope we can gradually pave the way toward a more enlightened military culture that respects the humanity and potential of all who wish to serve, regardless of any arbitrary number. This admittedly lofty goal is a challenge worth undertaking, a cause deserving of our most vigorous and virtuous efforts. And it is a journey well worth the tribulations if it brings us even incrementally closer to the just, equitable, and compassionate society we aspire to create.

Acknowledgements

My journey to write *The Ageless Call to Serve* has been a long and winding one, filled with unexpected turns and invaluable support from countless individuals. First and foremost, to my endeared wife, Dr. Tong Shen, I owe an immeasurable debt of gratitude. You have been my constant companion and source of inspiration throughout this journey. Your love, patience, and encouragement have sustained me through the challenges and triumphs of writing this book.

I must express my deepest gratitude to my collaborator and friend, JP Mark. JP first inspired me to embark on this literary adventure when we began working on "Journey to Ithaca," a memoir of my travels. Although that project took a different turn, it ultimately led me to Casemate Publishers and the birth of this book. JP, your unwavering support and belief in my story have been instrumental in bringing this work to life.

I am profoundly grateful to the many individuals who generously shared their stories and insights with me through interviews: Admiral Dennis McCoy, MAJ Benjamin Catlin, formerly CPT, Jeffrey Bamberg, formerly LTC, Crile Doscher, MD, LTC Robert J. Schneider, MA, PhD, COL Marty Strones, COL Ron Critsen, COL Richard L. Schneider, MD, formerly CPL, John Musgrave, COL David Siegel, and General Ralph Smith, Jr., MD—your candid and heartfelt contributions have enriched this book immensely.

I also wish to acknowledge the many others who must remain anonymous but whose honest and generous sharing has been equally invaluable.

A special thank you goes to Barbara Stoebner, whose unwavering support and guidance were instrumental in helping me join the U.S.

Army in 2003 at the age of 63. Barb, your belief in me and your tireless efforts to navigate the complexities of the joining process will forever be etched in my heart.

I am indebted to the incredible team at Casemate Publishers for their expertise and dedication in bringing this book to fruition. Ruth Sheppard, Elke Morice-Atkinson, Tracey Mills, Daniel Yesilonis, Declan Ingram, and the many others who worked tirelessly on the editing, cover design, proofreading, indexing, and countless other tasks—your professionalism and commitment to excellence have been genuinely inspiring.

Finally, I wish to express my heartfelt appreciation to the countless individuals who have touched my life and shaped my journey in big and small ways. To my fellow service members, the military mental health professionals, and the many others who have supported me along the way—your kindness, wisdom, and camaraderie have left an indelible mark on my heart.

Writing *The Ageless Call to Serve* has been a transformative experience that would not have been possible without the collective support and generosity of so many remarkable individuals. To each and every one of you, I offer my deepest gratitude and my promise to continue advocating for the mental well-being of our brave service members, regardless of their age.

With profound appreciation,
Lanny Snodgrass

Bibliography

Books

Bartetzko, R. (2018). *The Bosnian War: Memoirs of a Mujahid*. Mango Media Inc.

Borden, M. (1929). *The Forbidden Zone*. Hesperus Press Limited.

Bowlby, J. (1969). *Attachment and Loss: Volume 1—Attachment*. Basic Books.

Chamayou, G. (2015). *A Theory of the Drone*. New York: The New Press.

Connell, R. W. (1995). *Masculinities*. University of California Press.

Cross, C. R. (2010). *Room Full of Mirrors: A Biography of Jimi Hendrix*. London: Sceptre.

Dupuy, T. N. (2013). The Encyclopedia of Military History. HarperCollins.

Dursun, S. and Sudom, K. (2009). *Impacts of Military Life on Families: Results from the Perstempo Survey of Canadian Forces Spouses*. Defence R&D Canada.

Fell, J. (2020). *On this Day in History, Sh!t Went Down*. Calgary, Alberta: BFW Publishing.

Freeman, M. (2016). *From Failing Hands to Fighting Chance: How Military Service Changed My Life*. MICHAEL FREEMAN.

Galloway, J. L. and Moore, H. G. (1992). *We Were Soldiers Once ... And Young*. Random House.

Gillath, O., Karantzas, G. C., and Fraley, R. C. (2016). *Adult Attachment: A Concise Introduction to Theory and Research*. London: Academic Press.

Hanson, V. D. (2021). *The Dying Citizen*. Basic Books.

Herman, J. (1997). *Trauma and Recovery*. Basic Books.

Higonnet, M. R. (2001). *Nurses at the Front: Writing the Wounds of the Great War*. Harvard University Press.

Johnson, S. (1778). *The Idler*. J. Newbery.

Katz, L. S. (2016). *Treating Military Sexual Trauma*. New York: Springer Publishing Company.

Kübler-Ross, E. (1969). *On Death and Dying*. Macmillan Publishing Co.

La Motte, E. N. (2019). *The Backwash of War: An Extraordinary American Nurse in World War I*. Baltimore, MD: Johns Hopkins University Press.

Lewis, M. (2017). *The Undoing Project: A Friendship That Changed Our Minds*. W. W. Norton & Company.

Liebert, J. and Birnes, W. J. (2013). *Wounded Minds: Understanding and Solving the Growing Menace of Post-Traumatic Stress Disorder*. New York: Skyhorse Publishing.

Mason, P. H. C. (1990). *Recovering From the War*. Penguin Books Ltd.

McPherson, J. M. (1998). *Battle Cry of Freedom, The Civil War Era*. Oxford University Press.

Morris, D. J. (2015). *The Evil Hours: A Biography of Post-Traumatic Stress Disorder*. Eamon Dolan/Houghton Mifflin Harcourt.

Musgrave, J. (2021). *The Education of Corporal John Musgrave*. Knopf Publishing.

Nicholson, H. (2004). *Medieval Warfare: Theory and Practice of War in Europe, 300–1500*. Basingstoke: Palgrave Macmillan.

Rodger, N. A. M. (2004). *The Command of the Ocean: A Naval History of Britain 1649–1815*. W. W. Norton & Company.

Salerno, S. and Shields, D. (2013). *Salinger*. New York: Simon & Schuster.

Salinger, D. S. (2021). *Salinger*. New York: Simon & Schuster.

Sherman, W. T. (2016). *The Collected Works of William Tecumseh Sherman* (Vol. 1). Library of Alexandria.

Stouffer, J. (2015). *Intangible Friction: Addressing the Primary Cause of America's Military Recruiting Crisis*. Naval Postgraduate School Monterey, CA.

Strong, E. K. (1943). *Vocational Interests of Men and Women*. Stanford University Press.

Tonder, F. (1981). *The Children's War: The Second World War Through the Eyes of Children*. Viking Press.

Sullivan, H. S. (1953). *The Interpersonal Theory of Psychiatry*. W. W. Norton & Company.

Taylor, P., Parker, K., Morin, R., Patten, E., and Brown, A. (2014). *The Next America*. Pew Research Center.

Ursano, R. J., Fullerton, C. S., Weisaeth, L., and Raphael, B. (2007). *Textbook of Disaster Psychiatry*. Cambridge University Press.

Wandrey, J. (1989). *Bedpan Commando*. Holland, OH: Elmore Publishing.

Articles

Anderson, G. S., Litzenberger, R., and Plecas, D. (2002). "Physical evidence of police officer stress." *Policing: An International Journal of Police Strategies & Management*, 25(2), 399–420.

Aschbacher, K., O'Donovan, A., Wolkowitz, O. M., Dhabhar, F. S., Su, Y., and Epel, E. (2013). "Good stress, bad stress, and oxidative stress: insights from anticipatory cortisol reactivity." *Psychoneuroendocrinology*, 38(9), 1698–1708.

Asghar, M. (2017). "War & the Millennial Generation." *Harvard International Review*, 38(2), 20.

Baker, S., Fagan, S., Fischer, E., Janda, E., and Cove, L. (1967). "Impact of father absence on personality factors of boys: An evaluation of the family's adjustment." *American Journal of Orthopsychiatry*, 37, 269.

Bateman, T. (2023), "Tracking Military Recruiter Abuse." afsc.org. tracking military recruiters abuse, July 10, 2023.

Barlow, D. H., Elkins, G. R., and Barlow, A. K. H. (2007). "Effects of hypnotic drugs for prolonged mental health experience therapy of PTSD features." *Journal of Anxiety Disorders*, 21(8), 993–1002.

Barr, A. (2018). "Fighting for education: Veterans and financial aid." *Journal of Labor Economics*, 36(3), 923–961.

"Basic Training PFT Requirements." Military.com. Retrieved from https://www.military.com/military-fitness/army-fitness-requirements/army-basic-training-pft.

Bearce, D. (2020). "Military recruiters, skills training, and the supply of enlisted personnel." *Defense and Peace Economics*, 1–16.

Bogue, J. (2013). "Hitting the books: My adventures studying veterans." *Research & Practice in Assessment*, 8, 97–100.

Bonanno, G. A. (2004). "Loss, trauma, and human resilience: Have we underestimated the human capacity to thrive after extremely aversive events?" *American Psychologist*, 59(1), 20–28.

Burns, C. and Brainerd, C. J. (2019). "Reevaluating the effect of overqualification on job satisfaction." *Personnel Psychology*, 72(1), 5–37.

Clark, C. (2021). "The impact of telework on military operations." *Joint Forces Quarterly*, 99, 17–23.

DeFazio, V. J. and Pascucci, N. J. (1984). "Return to Ithaca: A perspective on marriage and love in post-traumatic stress disorder." *Journal of Contemporary Pyschotherapy*, 13, 76–89.

Dohrenwend, B., Yager, T., and Adams, B. (2013). "Why Some Soldiers Develop PTSD While Others Don't." Association for Psychological Science, https://www.psychologicalscience.org/news/releases/why-some-soldiers-develop-ptsd-while-others-dont.html.

DiDonato, T. (2016). "The Best (and Worst) Ages for Couples to Get Married." Psychology Today. Retrieved from https://www.psychologytoday.com/us/blog/meet-catch-and-keep/201606/the-best-and-worst-ages-couples-get-married.

Doody, B. D., Robertson, L., Cox, K. M., Bogue, J., Egan, J., and Suma, K. M. (2021). "Pre-deployment programs for building resilience in military and frontline emergency service personnel." Cochrane Library. https://cochranelibrary.com/cdsr/doi/10.1002/14651858.CD013242.pub2/full.

Dutra, L., Grubbs, K., Greene, C., Trego, L. L., McCartin, T. L., Kloezeman, K., and Morland, L. (2010). "Women at war: Implications for mental health." *Journal of Trauma & Dissociation*, 11(2), 25–137.

Egendorf, A., Kadushin, C., Laufer, R. S., Rothbart, G., and Sloan, L. (1981). "Legacies of Vietnam: Comparative adjustment of veterans and their peers." Washington, D.C.: U.S. Government Printing Office.

Ekelhof, M. (2022). "Autonomous weapon systems under international humanitarian law." Academy Briefing No. 26. The Hague: Clingendael Institute.

Elder, G. H., Jr., and Clipp, E. C. (1989). "Combat experience and emotional health: Impairment and resilience in later life." *Journal of Personality*, 57, 311–341.

Flake, E. M., Davis, B. E., Johnson, P. L., and Middleton, L. S. (2009). "The psychosocial effects of deployment on military children." *Journal of Developmental and Behavioral Pediatrics*, 30, 271–278.

Fredrickson, B. L., Tugade, M. M., Waugh, C. E., and Larkin, G. R. (2003). "What good are terrorist attacks on the United States on September 11th, 2001." *Journal of Personality and Social Psychology*, 84(2), 365–376.

Frick, E., and Bogart, G. (1981). "Family and group therapy concurrent with rap groups for Vietnam veterans." *International Journal of Family Therapy*, 3(3), 213–231.

Friedman, M. J. (2015). "PTSD History and Overview. U.S. Department of Veterans Affairs." Retrieved from https://www.ptsd.va.gov/professional/treat/essentials/history_ptsd.asp.

Frueh, B. C., Elhai, J. D., Monnier, J., Hamner, M. B., and Knapp, R. G. (2004). "Symptom patterns and comorbidity of dissociation in combat veterans with PTSD." *Journal of Trauma & Dissociation*, 5(2), 71–82.

Getty, M., (2023). "Putin turns to his dad's army as veterans of 70 face call-up to Ukraine." *The Times*. Retrieved from https://www.thetimes.co.uk/article/putin-nuclear-threat-war-russia-ukraine-kremlin-ftdpq|7qs.

Gibbs, D. A., Martin, S. L., Kupper, L. L., and Johnson, R. E. (2007). "Child maltreatment in enlisted soldiers' families during combat-related deployments." *JAMA*, 298, 528–535.

Glass-Coffin, B. (2019). "Veterans' experiences using post-9/11 G.I. bill benefits to attend for-profit educational institutions" (Order No. 13880701). Available from ProQuest Dissertations & Theses Global. (2240063106).

Glover, H. J. (1988). "Guilt that Combat Veterans Suffer." *Journal of Mental Disorders*, 172, 393–397.

Greene, T., Lahav, Y., Kanat-Maymon, Y., and Solomon, Z. (2020). "The role of personal growth in predicting mental health among veterans exposed to war captivity and torture." *Psychiatry Research*, 284, 112703

Hawkins, M. L. (2016). "Transformative Military Service: Turning Adversity into Growth." ProQuest LLC.

Heath, P. J., Seidel, J. A., Vogel, D. L., and Kruse, S. (2017). "Stigma, barriers, and reluctance to seek treatment for mental health problems in the military: A review of the literature." *Journal of Cognitive Psychotherapy*, 31(3), 234–262.

Henry, M., Watt, R., Rosenthal, L., and Shivji, A. (2017). "The 2017 Annual Homeless Assessment Report (AHAR) to Congress." The U.S. Department of Housing and Urban Development. Retrieved from https://www.huduser.gov/portal/sites/default/files/pdf/2017-AHAR-Part-1.pdf.

Herman, J. L. (1992). "Complex PTSD: A syndrome in survivors of prolonged and repeated trauma." *Journal of traumatic stress*, 5(3), 377–391.

Herringa, R. J., Burghy, C. A., Stodola, D. E., Fox, M. E., Davidson, R. J., and Essex, M. J. (2016). "Enhanced prefrontal-amygdala connectivity following childhood adversity as a protective mechanism against internalizing in adolescence." *Biological psychiatry: cognitive neuroscience and neuroimaging*, 1(4), 326–334.

Hoge, C. W. (2004). "Combat duty in Iraq and Afghanistan, mental health problems, and barriers to care." *New England Journal of Medicine*, 351(1), 13–22.

Hoge, C. W., Auchterlonie, J. L., and Milliken, C. S. (2006). "Mental health problems, use of mental health services, and attrition from military service after returning from deployment to Iraq or Afghanistan." *JAMA*, 295(9), 1023–1032.

Johnson, S. B., Blum, R. W., and Giedd, J. N. (2009). "Adolescent maturity and the brain: the promise and pitfalls of neuroscience research in adolescent health policy." *Journal of Adolescent Health*, 45(3), 216–221.

Kang, H. K., Bullman, T. A., Smolenski, D. J., Skopp, N. A., Gahm, G. A., and Reger, M. A. (2015). "Suicide risk among 1.3 million veterans who were on active duty during the Iraq and Afghanistan wars." *Annals of Epidemiology*, 25(2), 96–100.

Kelley, M. L., Hock, E., Smith, K. M., Jarvis, M. S., Bonney, J. F., and Gaffney, M. A. (2001). "Internalizing and externalizing behavior of children with enlisted Navy mothers experiencing military-induced separation." *Journal of the American Academy of Child and Adolescent Psychiatry*, 40, 464–471.

Kemp, J. and Bossarte, R. (2012). "Suicide Data Report: 2012." U.S. Department of Veterans Affairs. Retrieved from https://www.va.gov/opa/docs/suicide-data-report-2012-final.pdf.

Kessler, R. C. and Ursano, R. J. (2011). "Prevalence and Mental Health Correlates of Suicidal Ideation and Behaviors among Active Component Army Soldiers." National Institute of Mental Health.

Koenig, C. J., Maguen, S., Monroy, J. D., Mayott, L., and Seal, K. H. (2014). "Facilitating culture-centered communication between health care providers and veterans transitioning from military deployment to civilian life." *Patient Education and Counseling*, 95(3), 414–420.

Krediet, E., Bostoen, T., Breetsema, J., van Schagen, A., and Passie, T. (2020). "Reviewing the Potential of Psychedelics for the Treatment of PTSD." International Journal of Neuropsycho-pharmacology, 23(6), 385–405.

Lazalde, W. D. (2020). "The duty of operators: ethics of remote weapons." *Military Review*, 100(3), 28–38.

LeardMann, C. A., Matsuno, R. K., Boyko, T. M., Reger, M. A., and Hoge, C.W. (2021). "Association of Combat Experiences with Suicide Attempts Among Active-Duty U.S. Service Members." *JAMA Network Open*. DOI:10.1001/jamanetworkopen.2020.36065.

Leppin, A. L., Bora, P. R., Tilburt, J. C., Gionfriddo, M. R., Zeballos-Palacios, C., Dulohery, M. M., Sood, A., Erwin, P. J., Brito, J. P., Boehmer, K. R., and Montori, V. M. (2014). "The efficacy of resiliency training programs: a systematic review and meta-analysis of randomized trials." *PloS One*, 9(10), e111420.

Lester, P. and Flake, E. (2013). "How wartime military service affects children and families." *The Future of Children*, 23(2), 121–141.

Litz, B. T., Stein, N., Delaney, E., Lebowitz, L., Nash, W. P., Silva, C., and Maguen, S. (2009). "Moral injury and moral repair in war veterans: A preliminary model and intervention strategy." *Clinical Psychology Review*, 29(8), 695–706.

Lowe, K. N., Adams, K. S., Browne, B. L., and Hinkle, K. T. (2012). "Impact of military deployment on family relationships." *Journal of Family Studies*, 18(1), 17–27.

Maguen, S., Luxton, D. D., Skopp, N. A., Gahm, G. A., Reger, M. A., Metzler, T. J., and Marmar, C. R. (2011). "Killing in combat, mental health symptoms, and suicidal ideation in Iraq war veterans." *Journal of Anxiety Disorders*, 25(4), 563–567.

Maguen, S. and Norman, S. B. (2022). "Moral Injury." PTSD Research Quarterly, 33(1), 1–9.

Mahnken, T., Frazier, J., and Maiolo, J. (2019). "Redefining the Role of the Strategist." *Naval War College Review*, 72(2), 95.

Maier, S. U., Makwana, A. B., and Hare, T. A. (2015). "Acute stress impairs self-control in goal-directed choice by altering multiple functional connections within the brain's decision circuits." *Neuron*, 87(3), 621–631.

Marmar, C. R., McCaslin, S. E., Metzler, T. J., Best, S., Weiss, D. S., Fagan, J., Liberman, A., Pole, N., Otte, C., Yehuda, R., Mohr, D., and Neylan, T. (2006). "Predictors of post-traumatic stress in police and other first responders." *Annals of the New York Academy of Sciences*, 1071, 1–18.

Martin, M., Sasser, T., Burton, J., et al. (2017). "The drone deficit: Traditional war and the psychology of telewar." *The Lancet Psychiatry*, 4(11), 831–832.

McAleer, P. (2015). "Mandatory national service: Creating generations of civic minded citizens." *Advances in Applied Sociology*, 5(5), 285–294.

Meadows, S. O., Tanielian, T., Karney, B. R., Schell, T. L., Griffin, B. A., Jaycox, L. H., Friedman, E. M., Trail, T. E., Beckman, R. L., Marsella, A. J., Coughlin, R., Derr, M. K., Andrews, A., DeLeon, P., Brinson, J., and Borah, E. V. (2017). "The Deployment Life Study: Methodological overview and baseline sample description." *Rand Health Quarterly*, 7(1), 1–7.

Merchant, N. (2014). "Declining Enrollment in Military Academies and ROTC: What Are the Consequences?" *Journal Of Military and Strategic Studies*, 15(3).

Morgan, J. (2022). "Why veterans are ideal entrepreneurs." jpmorgan.com. Retrieved from https://www.jpmorgan.com/insights/business/business-planning/what-makes-veterans-good-entrepreneurs.

Myers, M. (2000). "Qualitative research and the generalizability question: Standing firm with Proteus." *The Qualitative Report*, 4(3), 9.

Nichter, B., Holliday, R., Monteith, L. L., Na, P. J., Hill, M. L., Kline, A. C., Norman, S. B., and Pietrzak, R. H. (2022). "Military sexual trauma in the United States: Results from a population-based study." *Journal of Affective Disorders*, 306, 19–27.

Nock, M. K., Borges, G., Bromet, E. J., Cha, C. B., Kessler, R. C., and Lee, S. (2008). "Suicide and Suicidal Behaviors." PubMed Central. Retrieved from https://www.ncbi.nlm.nkh.gov/articles/PMC2576496/.

Onion, A., Sullivan, M., Mullen, M., and Zapat, C. (2010). "This Day in History-Jimi Hendrix born." https://www.history.com/this-day-in-history/jimi-hendrix-born.

Park, N. (2011). "Military children and families: Strengths and challenges during peace and war." *American Psychologist*, 66(1), 65–72.

Paul, N. A., Stanton, S. J., Greeson, J. M., Smoski, M. J., and Wang, L. (2013). "Psychological and neural mechanisms of trait mindfulness in reducing depression vulnerability." *Social cognitive and affective neuroscience*, 8(1), 56–64.

Perales, R., Shaban-Nejad, A., Michalowski, W., and Buckeridge, D. L. (2021). "The Missing Soldiers: Assessing the Impact of the COVID-19 Pandemic on Military Forces and Veterans via Absenteeism in the Health System." *JMIR Public Health and Surveillance*, 7(3), e25849.

Pincus, S. H., House, R., Christenson, J., and Adler, L. E. (2001). "The emotional cycle of deployment: A military family perspective." *U.S. Army Medical Department Journal*, 4/5/6, 15–23.

Principi, A., Chiatti, C., Lamura, G., and Frerichs, F. (2012). "The engagement of older volunteers in traditional volunteering activities." *International Journal of Manpower*, 33(2), 104–122.

Protect Our Defenders. (2018). "Fact Sheet: Military Sexual Violence." Retrieved from https://www.protectourdefenders.com/factsheet/.

Reger, M. A., Smolenski, D. J., Skopp, N. A., Metzger-Abamukong, M. J., Kang, H. K., Bullman, T. A., Perdue, S., and Gahm, G. A. (2015). "Risk of suicide among US military service members following Operation Enduring Freedom or Operation Iraqi Freedom deployment and separation from the US military." *JAMA Psychiatry*, 72(6), 561–569.

Rivers, C. and Barnett, R. (2016). "Older workers can be more reliable and productive than their younger counter parts." Vox. Retrieved from https://www.vox.com/2016/10/18/12427494/old-aging-high-tech.

Roulo, C. (2013). "Defense Department expands women's combat role." American Forces Press Service. Retrieved from https://www.jble.af.mil/News/Article-Display/Article257998/defense-department-expands-womens-combat-role/.

Rudd, M. D., Goulding, J., and Bryan, C. J. (2011). "Student veterans: A national survey exploring psychological symptoms and suicide risk." *Professional Psychology: Research and Practice*, 42(5), 354.

Russo, S. J., Murrough, J. W., Han, M. H., Charney, D. S., and Nestler, E. J. (2012). "Neurobiology of resilience." *Nature Neuroscience*, 15(11), 1475–1484.

Rutter, M. (2000). "Resilience Reconsidered: Conceptual Considerations, Empirical Findings, and Policy Implications." *Handbook of Early Childhood Intervention*, 651–682.

Saini, R. K., Raju, M. S. V. K., and Chail, A. (2021). "Cry in the Sky: Psychological impact on drone operators." *Industrial Psychiatry Journal*, 30(Suppl 1), S15–S19.

Schneider, R. J. and Gilley, M. (1984). "Military Families and Combat Readiness in USAREUR." Washington, D.C.: Walter Reed Army Institute of Research. Unpublished technical report.

Schnurr, P. P., Lunney, C. A., and Sengupta, A. (2001). "Risk factors for the development versus maintenance of post-traumatic stress disorder." *Journal of Traumatic Stress*, 17(2), 85–95.

Scholtz, S. (2013). "Hypnotherapy as adjunct therapy in a case of post-traumatic stress disorder: A clinical report." *American Journal of Psychotherapy*, 67(3), 269–277.

Schulmeister, C. (2021). "Veteran experiences with the military to civilian transition: A phenomenological study." ProQuest Dissertations Publishing.

Shea, M. T., Reddy, M. K., Tyrka, A. R., and Sevin, E. (2013). "Risk factors for post-deployment posttraumatic stress disorder in National Guard/Reserve veterans of the Iraq War." *Psychiatry Research*, 210(1), 115–119.

Shefrick, B. M. (2018). "Veterans' experiences using post-9/11 G.I. bill benefits to attend proprietary educational institutions" (Order No. 10843397). Available from ProQuest Dissertations & Theses Global. (2166656178).

Sherman, W. T., "War Is Hell: William Tecumseh Sherman, Atlanta, and the March to the Sea," found in Ohio Memory, September 1, 2017. Ohio History Connection Selections, State Library of Ohio Historical Documents. Retrieved from https://ohiomemory.ohiohistory.org/archives/3447.

Shiner, B., D'Amico, S., John O. P., Brooks L., and Goldberg, B. (2022). "Factors associated with suicide risk in a population-based sample of post-9/11 Veterans." *Journal of Affective Disorders*, 300, 262–270.

Sisk, R. (2024). "The Military Recruiting Outlook Is Grim Indeed. Loss of Public Confidence, Political Attacks and the Economy Are All Taking a Toll." Retrieved in https://www.military.com/daily-news/2024/01/uphill-battle-boost-recruiting-military-faces-falling-public-confidence-political-attacks-economic.html.

Skomsvold, P., Radford, A. W., and Berkner, L. (2011). "Six-Year Attainment, Persistence, Transfer, Retention, and Withdrawal Rates of Students Who Began Postsecondary Education in 2003–04." Web Tables. NCES 2011-152. National Center for Education Statistics.

Smith, B. W., Dalen, J., Wiggins, K., Tooley, E., Christopher, P., and Bernard, J. (2008). "The brief resilience scale: assessing the ability to bounce back." Pubmed. Retrieved from https://pubmed.ncbi.nlm.nih.gov/18696313/.

Sogomonyan, F. and Cooper, J. L. (2010). "Trauma faced by children of military families: What every policymaker should know." National Center for Children in Poverty, Columbia University Publication.

Stanton, M. (2004). "Iraq Coalition Casualty Count." iCasualties.org. Retrieved from https://icasualties.org.

Steinberg, L., and Ritzmann, R. F. (1990). "A living systems approach to understanding the concept of stress resistance in development." *Behavioral Science*, 35(2), 138–146.

Thomas, M. M., Harpaz-Rotem, I., Tasi, J., Southwick, S. M., and Pietrzak, R. (2017). "Mental and Physical Health Conditions in U.S. Combat Veterans: Results From the National Health and Resilience in Veterans Study." Retrieved from Prim Care Companion CNS Discord, June 22.

Thorndike, E. L. (1920). "Intelligence and its uses." *Harper's Magazine*.

Tsai, J., Rosenheck, R. A., Kasprow, W. J., and McGuire, J. F. (2013). "Risk of Incarceration and Other Characteristics of Iraq and Afghanistan Era Veterans in State and Federal Prisons." *Psychiatric Services*, 64(1), 36–43.

Ursano, R. J., Fullerton, C. S., Vance, K., and Kao, T. C. (1999). "Posttraumatic Stress Disorder and Identification in Disaster Workers." *The American Journal of Psychiatry*, 156(3), 353–359.

Ursano, R. J., Goldenberg, M., Zhang, L., Carlton, J., Fullerton, C. S., Li, H., Johnson, L., and Benedek, D. (2010). "Posttraumatic stress disorder and traumatic stress: from bench to bedside, from war to disaster." *Annals of the New York Academy of Sciences*, 1208(1), 72–81.

"US doctor shortage: Pentagon plans unwise cuts in military doctors." *USA Today*. (July 18, 2019). Retrieved from https://www.usatoday.com/story/opinion/2019/07/18/military-doctors-trump-administration-staffing-cuts-congress-column/1753193001/.

Van der Werff, S. J., van den Berg, S. M., Pannekoek, J. N., Elzinga, B. M., and van der Wee, N. J. (2013). "Neuroimaging resilience to stress: a review." *Frontiers in behavioral neuroscience*, 7, 39.

Van Winkel, R., Wichers, M., Collip, D., Jacobs, N., Derom, C., Thiery, E., and Ryan, J. (2022). "Protocol for a randomised controlled trial to establish the efficacy of transcranial direct current stimulation as a treatment for depression in young people: the Resilience and Transcranial Electrical Neuromodulation (ReTiEN) study." *BMJ Open*, 12(5), e056478.

Wagnild, G. and Young, H. (1993). "Development and psychometric evaluation of the Resilience Scale." *Journal of Nursing Measurement*, 1(2), 165–178.

Waldron, K. (2008). "Troops unfit to fight sent into battle, report says." *New York Daily News*.

Warburton, D. and Bredin, S. D. (2016). "Reflections on Physical Activity and Health: What Should We Recommend?" *Canadian Journal of Cardiology*, 32(4), 495–504.

Wolfingr, N. (2015), "Want to Avoid Divorce? Wait to Get Married, But Not Too Long." Institute for Family Studies. Retrieved from https://ifstudies.org/blogwant-to-avoid-divorce-wait-to-get-married-but-not-too-long/.

Index